THE POCKET

Patriot

THE POCKET

Patriot

An Introduction
to the Principles
of Freedom

GEORGE GRANT

CUMBERLAND HOUSE
Nashville, Tennessee

Published by Cumberland House Publishing, Inc., 431 Harding Industrial Drive, Nashville, Tennessee 37211.

Cover design by Becky Brauner, Unlikely Suburban Design, Nashville, Tennessee.

Library of Congress Cataloging-in-Publication Data

Grant, George, 1954–
The pocket patriot : an introduction to the principles of
freedom / George Grant.
p. cm.
ISBN 1-58182-092-5 (paperback : alk. paper)
1. United States—History—Sources. I. Title.
E173.G79 2000
973—dc21   99-088254

Printed in the United States of America.

1 2 3 4 5 6 7 8—04 03 02 01 00

In Memoriam
Rus Walton

CONTENTS

INTRODUCTION

No people ought to feel greater obligations to celebrate the goodness of the Great Disposer of events and of the destiny of nations than the people of the United States. His kind providence originally conducted them to one of the best portions of the dwelling place allotted for the great family of the human race. He protected and cherished them under all the difficulties and trials to which they were exposed in their early days. Under His fostering care their habits, their sentiments, and their pursuits prepared them for a transition in due time to a state of independence and self-government.

James Madison

G. K. Chesterton once quipped that "America is the only nation in the world that is founded on a creed." Other nations find their identity and cohesion in ethnicity, or geography, or partisan ideology, or cultural tradition. But America was founded on certain ideas—ideas about freedom, about human dignity, and about social responsibility. It was this profound peculiarity that most struck Alexis de Tocqueville during his famous visit to this land at the beginning of the nineteenth century. He called it "American exceptionalism."

About the same time de Tocqueville penned his sage observations in his classic book, *Democracy in America,* educators in the fledgling republic began to realize that if their great experiment in liberty, their extraordinary American exceptionalism, were to be maintained over the course of succeeding generations, then an informed patriotism would have to be instilled in the hearts and minds of the young. Indeed, John Quincy Adams wrote, "Posterity: you will never know how much it has cost my generation to preserve your freedom. I hope you will make good use of it."

Thus, from the middle of the nineteenth century to the middle of the twentieth, rising citizens were presented with small handbooks—brief guides to the essential elements of the American creed. Pastors, statesmen, educators, and parents wanted to somehow pass on to posterity the moral and constitutional tools necessary to make good use of their freedom.

Over the past few years I have tried to collect a representative sample of such handbooks—scouring dusty antiquarian book shops, libraries, and academic collections whenever and wherever I could. Although they varied somewhat over the years in presentation, style, and format, it appears that each was designed to be an introductory and documentary record of the development, confirmation, and establishment of the exceptional American creed. They were offered to the ever-changing citizenry in the hope that the never-changing principles of freedom might be fully comprehended and defended against any and all incursions.

During the pivotal 1996 election season, I compiled and Cumberland House published an updated version of that vaunted tradition, *The Patriot's Handbook*. Containing a concise introduction to the foundational ideas, documents, events, and personalities of American freedom, it was a citizenship primer for a whole new generation of American patriots. But while that collection was quickly adopted into history and civics curricula all across the country, it was too large and bulky to be widely utilized outside the classroom. Thus, this much-abbreviated version has been prepared for the even more pivotal 2000 elections.

Alexis de Tocqueville has oft been quoted—perhaps apocryphally—saying, "I sought for the greatness and genius of America in her commodious harbors and her ample rivers, and it was not there; in her fertile fields and boundless prairies, and it was not there; in her rich mines and her vast world commerce, and it was not there. Not until I went to the churches of America and heard her pulpits aflame with righteousness did I understand the secret of her genius and power. America is great because she is good and if America ever ceases to be good, America will cease to be great."

This very brief anthology of historical and citizenship resources is offered in the hope that the ideas that made America both great and good may once again become the common currency of our national life. It is offered in the

hope that the secret of our genius and power might be broad-
cast far and wide—and thus, essentially cease to be a secret.

Bannockburn College
Advent 1999

THE POCKET
Patriot

THE APOLOGIA OF COLUMBUS

*On October 12, 1492, when he stepped upon the shore of the little Caribbean island of San Salvador, Christopher Columbus ushered in a new age of exploration and settlement the likes of which the world had not ever seen. He also greatly contributed to the providential perspective of American history—a view that asserts the directing hand of Almighty God—through the publication of his **Book of Prophesies** some ten years later. This short excerpt gives a glimpse of that providential perspective and captures the essence of the Admiral of the Ocean Sea's extraordinary world-view.*

At a very early age I went to sea and have continued navigating until today. The art of sailing is favorable for anyone who wants to pursue knowledge of this world's secrets. I have already been at this business for forty years. I have sailed all the waters which up to now, have been navigated. I have had dealings and conversation with learned people—clergymen and laymen, Latins and Greeks, Jews and Moors, and with many others of other sects.

I found our Lord very well disposed toward this, my desire, and he gave me the spirit for it. He prospered me in seamanship and supplied me with the necessary tools of astronomy, as well as geometry and arithmetic and ingenuity of manual skill to draw spherical maps which show cities, rivers and mountains, islands and ports—everything in its proper place.

I have seen and put into study to look into all the Scriptures, cosmography, histories, chronicles, philosophy, and other arts, which our Lord has opened to understanding, so that it became clear to me that it was feasible to navigate from here to the Indies; and He unlocked within me the determination to execute the idea. And I came to the Sovereigns of Castile and Aragon with this ardor. All those who heard about my enterprise rejected it with laughter, scoffing at me. Neither the sciences which I mentioned, nor the authoritative citations from them, were of any avail. In only the sovereigns remained faith and constancy. Who doubts that this illumination was from the Holy Spirit? I attest that He, with marvelous rays of light, consoled me through the holy and sacred Scriptures, a strong and clear testimony, with forty four books of the Old Testament, and four Gospels with twenty three Epistles of those blessed Apostles, encouraging me to proceed, and, continually, without ceasing for a moment, they inflame me with a sense of great urgency.

Our Lord wished to perform the clearest work of providence in this matter—the voyage to the Indies—to console me and others in this matter of the Holy Temple: I have spent seven years in the royal court arguing the case with many persons of such authority and learned in all the arts, and in the end they concluded that all was idle nonsense, and with this they gave up the enterprise; yet the outcome was to be the fulfillment of what our Redeemer Jesus Christ said beforehand through the mouth of the prophets.

And so the prophesy has been made manifest.

AMERICAN SPIRIT

From the time of the earliest explorations of the Norse along Ultima Thule and the conquistadors in the Caribbean to the settlements of the pioneers in Virginia and the Pilgrims in Massachusetts, Americans have always been proud of their courageous heritage and lineage. That unique legacy is celebrated in this popular nineteenth-century verse by Arthur Cleveland Coxe.

Oh, who has not heard of the Northmen of yore,
How flew, like the sea-bird, their sails from the shore;
How, westward, they stayed not till, breasting the brine,
They hailed Narragansett, the land of the vine!

Then the war-songs of Rollo, his pennon and glaive,
Were heard as they danced by the moon-lighted wave,
And their golden-haired wives bore them sons of the soil,
While raged with the redskins their feud and turmoil.

And who has not seen, 'mid the summer's gay crowd,
That old pillared tower of their fortalice proud,
How it stands solid proof of the sea chieftains' reign
Ere came with Columbus those galleys of Spain!

Twas a claim for their kindred: an earnest of sway,
By the stout-hearted Cabot made good in its day;
Of the Cross of St. George, on the Chesapeake's tide,
Where lovely Virginia arose like a bride.

Came the Pilgrims with Winthrop; and, saint of the West,
Came Robert of Jamestown, the brave and the blest;
Came Smith, the bold rover, and Rolfe—with his ring,
To wed sweet Matoaka, child of a king.

Undaunted they came, every peril to dare,
Of tribes fiercer far than the wolf in his lair;
Of the wild irksome woods, where in ambush they lay;
Of their terror by night and their arrow by day.

And so where our capes cleave the ice of the poles,
Where groves of the orange scent sea-coast and shoals,
Where the froward Atlantic uplifts its last crest,
Where the sun, when he sets, seeks the East from the West;

The clime that from ocean to ocean expands,
The fields to the snowdrifts that stretch from the sands,
The wilds they have conquered of mountain and plain;
Those Pilgrims have made them fair Freedom's domain.

And the bread of dependence if proudly they spurned,
Twas the soul of their fathers that kindled and burned,
Twas the blood of old Saxon within them that ran;
They held—to be free is the birthright of man.

So oft the old lion, majestic of mane,
sees cubs of his cave breaking loose from his reign;
Unmeet to be his if they braved not his eye,
He gave them the spirit his own to defy.

FLAWLESS HEART

The great critic and editor James Russell Lowell wrote a number of poems that bear testimony of the tremendous courage and tenacity of America's earliest settlers. This particular verse of his was a favorite during the halcyon days of optimism at the end of the nineteenth century.

Flawless his Heart and tempered to the core
Who, beckoned by the forward-leaning wave,
First left behind him the firm-footed shore,
And, urged by every nerve of sail and oar,
Steered for the Unknown which gods to mortals gave,
Of thought and action the mysterious door,
Bugbear of fools, a summons to the brave:
Strength found he in the unsympathizing sun,
And strange stars from beneath the horizon won,
and the dumb ocean pitilessly grave:
High-hearted surely he;
But bolder they who first off-cast
Their moorings from the habitable Past
And ventured chartless on the sea
Of storm-engendering Liberty:
For all earth's width of waters is a span,

And their convulsed existence mere repose,
Matched with the unstable heart of man,
Shoreless in wants, mist-girt in all it knows,
Open to every wind of sect or clan,
And sudden-passionate in ebbs and flows.

THE MAYFLOWER COMPACT

*Drafted and signed on board the **Mayflower** as that ship approached Cape Cod on November 11, 1620, this document is regarded as one of the most important in American history. It proves the determination of the small group of English separatist Christians to live under a rule of law, based on the consent of the people, and to set up their own civil government. The parchment has long since disappeared—the current text was first printed in London in 1622 in a pamphlet generally known as **Mourt's Relation**, which contained extracts from the fledgling colony's journals and histories. In an oration delivered at Plymouth in 1802, John Quincy Adams declared that it was "perhaps the only instance, in human history, of that positive, original social compact, which speculative philosophers have imagined as the only legitimate source of government." Thus, the Pilgrim Fathers had anticipated the social contract 70 years before John Locke and 140 years before Jean Jacques Rousseau.*

In the name of God Amen. We whose names are underwriten, the loyal subjects of our dread sovereign Lord King James by the grace of God, of Great Britain, France, and Ireland king, defender of the faith, etceteras.

Having undertaken, for the glory of God, and advancements of the Christian faith and honor of our king

& country, a voyage to plant the first colony in the Northern parts of Virginia, doe by these presents solemnly &
mutually in the presence of God, and one of another,
covenant & combine our selves together into a civil body
politick; for our better ordering, & preservation & further-
ance of the ends aforesaid; and by virtue hearof to enact,
constitute, and frame such just & equal laws, ordinances,
Acts, constitutions, and offices, from time to time, as shall
be thought most meet and convenient for the general good
of the Colony: unto which we promise all due submission
and obedience.

In witness whereof we have hereunder subscribed our
names at Cape Cod the eleventh of November, in the year
of the reign of our sovereign Lord King James of England,
France, and Ireland the eighteenth and of Scotland the
fifty fourth, Anno Dominie, 1620.

FIVE KERNELS OF CORN

The first few winters in the New World were treacherous for the new colonists. In the Plymouth Colony, the settlers died in droves from both sickness and starvation. In this verse, the necessity of rationing the meager food resources is set alongside the abundant moral reserves of the people. Long a part of the traditional New England holiday tradition—before the turkey is carved, each member of the family is served a mere five kernels of corn after which this inspiring poem by Hezekiah Butterworth is recited— the remembrance of Plymouth has become a symbol of the incredible blessing of this land.

Twas the year of the famine in Plymouth of old,
    The ice and the snow from the thatched roofs had
        rolled;
Through the warm purple skies steered the geese o'er the
        seas,
    And the woodpeckers tapped in the clocks of the trees;
And the boughs on the slopes to the south winds lay bare,
    And dreaming of summer, the buds swelled in the air.
The pale Pilgrims welcomed each reddening morn;
    There were left but for rations Five Kernels of Corn.

Five Kernels of Corn!
Five Kernels of Corn!
But to Bradford a feast were Five Kernels of Corn!

"Five Kernels of Corn! Five Kernels of Corn!
    Ye people, be glad for Five Kernels of Corn!"
So Bradford cried out on bleak Burial Hill,
    And the thin women stood in their doors, white and
        still.
"Lo, the harbor of Plymouth rolls bright in the Spring,
    The maples grow red, and the wood robins sing,
The west wind is blowing, and fading the snow
    And the pleasant pines sing, and arbutuses blow.
    Five Kernels of Corn!
    Five Kernels of Corn!
To each one be given Five Kernels of Corn!"

O Bradford of Austerfield haste on thy way.
    The west winds are blowing o'er Provincetown Bay,
The white avens bloom, but the pine domes are chill,
    And new graves have furrowed Precisioners' Hill!
"Give thanks, all ye people, the warm skies have come,
    The hilltops are sunny, and green grows the holm,
And the trumpets of winds, and the white March is gone,
    And ye still have left you Five Kernels of Corn.
    Five Kernels of Corn!
    Five Kernels of Corn!
Ye have for Thanksgiving Five Kernels of Corn!

"The raven's gift eat and be humble and pray,

A new light is breaking, and Truth leads your way;
One taper a thousand shall kindle: rejoice
That to you has been given the wilderness voice!"
O Bradford of Austerfield, daring the wave,
And safe though the sounding blasts leading the brave,
Of deeds such as thine was the free nation born,
And the festal world sings the "Five Kernels of Corn."
Five Kernels of Corn!
Five Kernels of Corn!
The nation gives thanks for Five Kernels of Corn!
To the Thanksgiving Feast bring Five Kernels of Corn!

AWAKEN

The Great Awakening touched every section of the colonial domains of England in the New World—from northernmost New England to southernmost Georgia. And its impact was enormous. Interestingly, this cultural and spiritual phenomenon was driven entirely by grassroots evangelism and community cooperation, as this famous verse by Lawrence Tribble illustrates.

One man awake,
    Awakens another.
The second awakens
    His next-door brother.
The three awake can rouse a town
    By turning
    The whole place
    Upside down.
The many awake
    Can make such a fuss
It finally awakens
    The rest of us.
One man up,
    With dawn in his eyes,
    Surely then
    Multiplies.

LIBERTY OR DEATH

This famous speech was delivered by Patrick Henry at Richmond's historic St. John's Church in the year before the signing of the Declaration of Independence. Henry was the first governor of the state of Virginia and a member of the First Continental Congress. His fiery call to arms against British oppression caused an immediate and rousing reaction—and it subsequently became one of the great clarion cries for freedom that circulated throughout all the colonies.

No man thinks more highly than I do of the patriotism, as well as abilities, of the very worthy gentlemen who have just addressed the House. But different men often see the same subjects in different lights; and, therefore, I hope that it will not be thought disrespectful to those gentlemen, if, entertaining as I do, opinions of a character very opposite to theirs, I shall speak forth my sentiments freely and without reserve. This is no time for ceremony. The question before the House is one of awful moment to this country. For my own part I consider it as nothing less than a question of freedom or slavery, and in proportion to the magnitude of the subject ought to be the freedom of the debate. It is only in this way that we can hope to arrive at truth and fulfill the great responsibility which we hold to God and our country. Should I keep back my opinions at such a time, through fear of giving offense, I should consider myself as guilty of treason toward my country and of an act of disloyalty toward the majesty of heaven, which I revere above all earthly kings.

It is natural to man to indulge in the illusions of hope. We are apt to shut our eyes against a painful truth and listen to the song of that siren, till she transforms us into beasts. Is this the part of wise men, engaged in a great and arduous struggle for liberty? Are we disposed to be of the number of those who, having eyes, see not, and having ears, hear not, the things which so nearly concern their temporal salvation? For my part, whatever anguish of spirit it may cost, I am willing to know the whole truth, to know the worst and to provide for it.

I have but one lamp by which my feet are guided, and that is the lamp of experience. I know of no way of judging of the future but by the past. And judging by the past, I wish to know what there has been in the conduct of the British ministry for the last ten years to justify those hopes with which gentlemen have been pleased to solace themselves and the House? Is it that insidious smile with which our petition has been lately received? Trust it not, sir; it will prove a snare to your feet. Suffer not yourselves to be betrayed with a kiss. Ask yourselves how this gracious reception of our petition comports with these warlike preparations which cover our waters and darken our land. Are fleets and armies necessary to a work of love and reconciliation? Have we shown our-selves so unwilling to be reconciled that force must be called in to win back our love?

Let us not deceive ourselves, sir. These are the imple-ments of war and subjugation, the last arguments to which kings resort. I ask gentlemen, sir, what means this martial array, if its purpose be not to force us to submission? Can gentlemen assign any other possible motives for it? Has Great Britain any enemy, in this quarter of the world, to call for all this accumulation of navies and armies? No, sir, she has none. They are meant for us; they can be meant for no other. They are sent over to bind and rivet upon us those chains which the British ministry have been so long forg-ing. And what have we to oppose to them? Shall we try argument? Sir, we have been trying that for the last ten years. Have we anything new to offer on the subject? Noth-ing. We have held the subject up in every light of which it is capable, but it has been all in vain. Shall we resort to entreaty and humble supplication? What terms shall we find which have not been already exhausted? Let us not, I beseech you, sir, deceive ourselves longer. Sir, we have done everything that could be done to avert the storm which is now coming on. We have petitioned; we have remon-strated; we have supplicated; we have prostrated ourselves before the tyrannical hands of the ministry and parliament. Our petitions have been slighted; our remonstrances have produced additional violence and insult; our supplications have been disregarded; and we have been spurned, with contempt, from the foot of the throne.

In vain, after these things, may we indulge the fond hope of peace and reconciliation. There is no longer any room for hope. If we wish to be free—if we mean to preserve inviolate those inestimable privileges for which we have been so long contending—if we mean not basely to abandon the noble struggle in which we have been so long engaged, and which we have pledged ourselves never to abandon until the glorious object of our contest shall be obtained, we must fight! I repeat it, sir, we must fight! An appeal to arms and to the God of Hosts is all that is left us!

They tell us, sir, that we are weak, unable to cope with so formidable an adversary. But when shall we be stronger? Will it be the next week, or the next year? Will it be when we are totally disarmed, and when a British guard shall be stationed in every house? Shall we gather strength by irresolution and inaction? Shall we acquire the means of effectual resistance by lying supinely on our backs and hugging the delusive phantom of hope, until our enemies shall have bound us hand and foot? Sir, we are not weak, if we make a proper use of the means which the God of nature hath placed in our power. Three millions of people, armed in the holy cause of liberty, and in such a country as that which we possess, are invincible by any force which our enemy can send against us. Besides, sir, we shall not fight our battles alone. There is a just God who presides over the destinies of nations, and who will raise friends to fight our battles for us. The battle, sir, is not to the strong alone; it is to the vigilant, the active, the brave. Besides, sir, we have no election. If we were base enough to desire it, it is now too late to retire from the contest. There is no retreat but in submission and slavery! Our chains are forged! Their clanking may be heard on the plains of Boston! The war is inevitable—and let it come! I repeat it, sir, let it come!

It is in vain, sir, to extenuate the matter. Gentlemen may cry, peace, peace!—but there is no peace. The war is actually begun! The next gale that sweeps from the north will bring to our ears the clash of resounding arms! Our brethren are already in the field! Why stand we here idle? What is it that gentlemen wish? What would they have? Is life so dear, or peace so sweet, as to be purchased at the price of chains and slavery? Forbid it, Almighty God! I know not what course others may take, but as for me: Give me liberty, or give me death!

PAUL REVERE'S RIDE

This tale, one of the most legendary in all the Founding Era, was set to verse by one of America's foremost poets, Henry Wadsworth Longfellow. It immediately became a popular anthem celebrating both the great valor of the revolutionaries and the great virtue of the revolutionary cause.

Listen, my children, and you shall hear
Of the midnight ride of Paul Revere
On the eighteenth of April, in Seventy-five;
Hardly a man is now alive
Who remembers that famous day and year.

He said to his friend, "If the British march
By land or sea from the town to-night,
Hang a lantern aloft in the belfry arch
Of the North Church tower as a signal light,
One, if by land, and two, if by sea;
And I on the opposite shore will be,
Ready to ride and spread the alarm
Through every Middlesex village and farm,
For the country folk to be up and to arm."

Then he said, "Good night!" and with muffled oar
Silently rowed to the Charlestown shore,

Just as the moon rose over the bay,
Where swinging wide at her moorings lay
The *Somerset,* British man-of-war;
A phantom ship, with each mast and spar
Across the moon like a prison bar
And a huge black hulk, that was magnified
By its own reflection in the tide.

Meanwhile, his friend, through alley and street,
Wanders and watches with eager ears,
Till in the silence around him he hears
The muster of men at the barrack door,
The sound of arms, and the tramp of feet,
And the measured tread of the grenadiers,
Marching down to their boats on the shore.

Then he climbed the tower of the Old North Church,
By the wooden stairs, with stealthy tread,
To the belfry-chamber overhead,
And startled the pigeons from their perch
On the sombre rafters, that round him made
Masses and moving shapes of shade,
By the trembling ladder, steep and tall,
To the highest window in the wall,
Where he paused to listen and look down
A moment on the roofs of the town,
And the moonlight flowing over all.

Beneath, in the churchyard, lay the dead,
In their night-encampment on the hill,

Wrapped in silence so deep and still
That he could hear, like a sentinel's tread,
The watchful night-wind, as it went
Creeping along from tent to tent,
And seeming to whisper, "All is well!"
A moment only he feels the spell
Of the place and the hour, and the secret dread
Of the lonely belfry and the dead;
For suddenly all his thoughts are bent
On a shadowy something far away,
Where the river widens to meet the bay,
A line of black that bends and floats
On the rising tide, like a bridge of boats.

Meanwhile, impatient to mount and ride,
Booted and spurred, with a heavy stride
On the opposite shore walked Paul Revere.
Now he patted his horse's side,
Now gazed at the landscape far and near,
Then, impetuous, stamped the earth,
And turned and tightened his saddle-girth;
But mostly he watched with eager search
The belfry-tower of the Old North Church,
As it rose above the graves on the hill,
Lonely and spectral and sombre and still.
And lo! as he looks, on the belfry's height
A glimmer, and then a gleam of light!
He springs to the saddle, the bridle he turns,

But lingers and gazes, till full on his sight
A second lamp in the belfry burns!

A hurry of hoofs in a village street,
A shape in the moonlight, a bulk in the dark,
And beneath, from the pebbles, in passing, a spark
Struck out by a steed flying fearless and fleet:
That was all! And yet, through the gloom and the light,
The fate of a nation was riding that night,
And the spark struck out by that steed, in his flight,
Kindled the land into flame with its heat.

He has left the village and mounted the steep,
And beneath him, tranquil and broad and deep,
Is the Mystic, meeting the ocean tides;
And under the alders that skirt its edge,
Now soft on the sand, now loud on the ledge,
Is heard the tramp of his steed as he rides.

It was twelve by the village clock,
When he crossed the bridge into Medford town.
He heard the crowing of the cock,
And the barking of the farmer's dog,
And felt the damp of the river fog,
That rises after the sun goes down.

It was one by the village clock,
When he galloped into Lexington.
He saw the gilded weathercock
Swim in the moonlight as he passed,

And the meeting-house windows, blank and bare,
Gaze at him with a spectral glare,
As if they already stood aghast
At the bloody work they would look upon.

It was two by the village clock,
When he came to the bridge in Concord town.
He heard the bleating of the flock,
And the twitter of birds among the trees,
And felt the breath of the morning breeze
Blowing over the meadows brown.
And one was safe and asleep in his bed
Who at the bridge would be first to fall,
Who that day would be lying dead,
Pierced by a British musket-ball.

You know the rest. In the books you have read,
How the British Regulars fired and fled,
How the farmers gave them ball for ball,
From behind each fence and farm-yard wall,
Chasing the red-coats down the lane,
Then crossing the fields to emerge again
Under the trees at the turn of the road,
And only pausing to fire and load.

So through the night rode Paul Revere;
And so through the night went his cry of alarm
To every Middlesex village and farm,—
A cry of defiance and not of fear,
A voice in the darkness, a knock at the door,

And a word that shall echo forevermore!
For, borne on the night-wind of the Past,
Through all our history, to the last,
In the hour of darkness and peril and need,
The people will waken and listen to hear
The hurrying hoof-beats of that steed,
And the midnight message of Paul Revere.

THE DIVINE SOURCE
OF LIBERTY

Samuel Adams was one of the firebrands of the Revolution. The founder of the Committees of Correspondence and the Sons of Liberty, he challenged the authority of the English to violate the common law tradition in the colonies and eventually led the armed resistance to the king's tyranny following the Boston Massacre. In this widely circulated verse, he detailed the standards for the American demand for freedom.

All temporal power is of God,
And the magistratal, His institution, laud,
To but advance creaturely happiness aubaud:

Let us then affirm the Source of Liberty.

Ever agreeable to the nature and will,
Of the Supreme and Guardian of all yet still
Employed for our rights and freedom's thrill:

Thus proves the only Source of Liberty.

Though our civil joy is surely expressed
Through hearth, and home, and church manifest,
Yet this too shall be a nation's true test:

To acknowledge the divine Source of Liberty.

THE DECLARATION
OF INDEPENDENCE

On June 9, 1776, the Continental Congress accepted a resolution of Virginia delegate Richard Henry Lee to appoint a committee to draft a declaration of secession from the dominions of the English king and Parliament. On June 29, the committee—composed of Thomas Jefferson, John Adams, Benjamin Franklin, Roger Sherman, and Robert Livingston—presented their draft for debate and a vote. Finally, on July 4, an amended version of that draft was accepted. The war that had been raging for more than a year had finally driven the reluctant revolutionaries to sever all ties with their motherland.

When in the course of human events, it becomes necessary for one people to dissolve the political bands which have connected them with another, and to assume among the powers of the earth the separate and equal station to which the laws of nature and of nature's God entitle them, a decent respect to the opinions of mankind requires that they should declare the causes which impel them to the separation.

We hold these truths to be self-evident: that all men are created equal, that they are endowed by their Creator with certain unalienable rights, that among these are life, liberty, and the pursuit of happiness. That to secure these rights, governments are instituted among men, deriving their just powers from the consent of the governed; that whenever any form of government becomes destructive of these ends, it is the right of the people to alter or to abolish it, and to institute new government, laying its foundation on such principles and organizing its powers in such form, as to them shall seem most likely to effect their safety and happiness.

Prudence, indeed, will dictate that governments long established should not be changed for light and transient causes; and accordingly all experience hath shown, that mankind are more disposed to suffer, while evils are sufferable, than to right themselves by abolishing the forms to which they are accustomed. But when a long train of abuses and usurpations, pursuing invariably the same object, evinces a design to reduce them under absolute despotism, it is their right, it is their duty, to throw off such government, and to provide new guards for their future security. Such has been the patient sufferance of these colonies; and such is now the necessity which constrains them to alter their former systems of government.

The history of the present king of Great Britain is a history of repeated injuries and usurpations, all having in direct object the establishment of an absolute tyranny over these states. To prove this, let facts be submitted to a candid world.

He has refused his assent to laws, the most wholesome and necessary for the public good.

He has forbidden his governors to pass laws of immediate and pressing importance, unless suspended in their operation till his assent should be obtained; and when so suspended, he has utterly neglected to attend to them.

He has refused to pass other laws for the accommodation of large districts of people, unless those people would relinquish the right of representation in the legislature, a right inestimable to them and formidable to tyrants only.

He has called together legislative bodies at places unusual, uncomfortable, and distant from the depository of their public records, for the sole purpose of fatiguing them into compliance with his measures.

He has dissolved representative houses repeatedly for opposing with manly firmness his invasions on the rights of the people.

He has refused for a long time, after such dissolutions, to cause others to be elected; whereby the legislative powers, incapable of annihilation, have returned to the people at large for their exercise; the state remaining in the meantime exposed to all the dangers of invasion from without, and convulsions within.

He has endeavored to prevent the population of these states; for that purpose obstructing the laws for naturalization of foreigners; refusing to pass others to encourage their migration hither, and raising the conditions of new appropriations of lands.

He has obstructed the administration of justice, by refusing his assent to laws for establishing judiciary powers.

He has made judges dependent on his will alone, for the tenure of their offices, and the amount and payment of their salaries.

He has erected a multitude of new offices, and sent hither swarms of officers to harass our people and eat out their substance.

He has kept among us, in times of peace, standing armies without the consent of our legislature.

He has affected to render the military independent of and superior to the civil power.

He has combined with others to subject us to a jurisdiction foreign to our constitution, and unacknowledged by our laws; giving his assent to their acts of pretended legislation:

For quartering large bodies of armed troops among us;

For protecting them, by a mock trial, from punishment for any murders which they should commit on the inhabitants of these states;

For cutting off our trade with all parts of the world;

For imposing taxes on us without our consent;

For depriving us, in many cases, of the benefits of trial by jury;

For transporting us beyond seas to be tried for pretended offenses;

For abolishing the free system of English laws in a neighboring province, establishing therein an arbitrary government, and enlarging its boundaries so as to render it at once an example and fit instrument for introducing the same absolute rule into these colonies;

For taking away our charters, abolishing our most valuable laws, and altering fundamentally the forms of our governments;

For suspending our own legislatures, and declaring themselves invested with power to legislate for us in all cases whatsoever.

He has abdicated government here by declaring us out of his protection and waging war against us.

He has plundered our seas, ravaged our coasts, burnt our towns, and destroyed the lives of our people.

He is at this time transporting large armies of foreign mercenaries to complete the works of death, desolation, and tyranny, already begun with circumstances of cruelty and perfidy scarcely paralleled in the most barbarous ages, and totally unworthy the head of a civilized nation.

He has constrained our fellow citizens taken captive on the high seas to bear arms against their country, to become the executioners of their friends and brethren, or to fall themselves by their hands.

He has excited domestic insurrections amongst us, and has endeavored to bring on the inhabitants of our frontiers, the merciless Indian savages, whose known rule of warfare is an undistinguished destruction of all ages, sexes, and conditions.

In every stage of these oppressions we have petitioned for redress in the most humble terms; our repeated petitions have been answered only by repeated injury. A prince, whose character is thus marked by every act which may define a tyrant, is unfit to be the ruler of a free people.

Nor have we been wanting in attention to our British brethren. We have warned them from time to time of attempts by their legislature to extend an unwarrantable jurisdiction over us. We have reminded them of the circumstances of our emigration and settlement here. We have appealed to their native justice and magnanimity, and we have conjured them by the ties of our common kindred to disavow these usurpations, which would inevitably interrupt our connections and correspondence. They too have been deaf to the voice of justice and of consanguinity. We must, therefore, acquiesce in the necessity which denounces our separation, and hold them, as we hold the rest of mankind, enemies in war, in peace, friends.

We, therefore, the representatives of the United States of America, in general congress assembled, appealing to the Supreme Judge of the world for the rectitude of our intentions, do, in the name and by authority of the good people of these colonies, solemnly publish and declare, that these united colonies are, and of right ought to be, free and independent states; that they are absolved from all allegiance to the British crown, and that all political connection between them and the state of Great Britain is, and ought to be, totally dissolved; and that as free and independent states they have full power to levy war, conclude peace, contract alliances, establish commerce, and to do all other acts and things which independent states may of right do. And for the support of this declaration, with a firm reliance on the protection of Divine Providence, we mutually pledge to each other our lives, our fortunes, and our *sacred* honor.

LEXINGTON

*As the Revolutionary War began, the ragtag American militia
fought with extraordinary courage and distinction. The first of
the battles was little more than a skirmish, yet it inspired a
"shot heard 'round the world" sense of national pride. In this
verse another of America's greatest historical poets, John
Greenleaf Whittier, re-creates the epic scene.*

No Berserk thirst of blood had they,
No battle-joy was theirs, who set
Against the alien bayonet
Their homespun breasts in that old day.

Their feet had trodden peaceful ways;
They loved not strife, they dreaded pain;
They saw not, what to us is plain,
That God would make man's wrath His praise.

No seers were they, but simple men;
Its vast results the future hid:
The meaning of the work they did
Was strange and dark and doubtful then.

Swift as their summons came they left
The plow mid-furrow standing still,

The half-ground corn grist in the mill,
The spade in earth, the axe in cleft.

They went where duty seemed to call,
They scarcely asked the reason why;
They only knew they could but die,
And death was not the worst of all!

Of man for man the sacrifice,
All that was theirs to give, they gave.
The flowers that blossomed from their grave
Have sown themselves beneath all skies.

Their death-shot shook the feudal tower,
And shattered slavery's chain as well
On the sky's dome, as on a bell,
Its echo struck the world's great hour.

That fateful echo is not dumb:
The nations listening to its sound
Wait, from a century's vantage-ground,
The holier triumphs yet to come.

The bridal time of Law and Love,
The gladness of the world's release,
When, war-sick, at the feet of Peace
The hawk shall nestle with the dove!

The golden age of brotherhood
Unknown to other rivalries
Than of the mild humanities,
And gracious interchange of good,

When closer strand shall lean to strand,
Till meet, beneath saluting flags,
The eagle of our mountain-crags,
The lion of our Motherland!

FOUNDING FATHERS

The Founding Era was replete with great men. At perhaps no other time in history have so many dynamic, gifted, and courageous leaders been simultaneously active in public affairs. The lives and careers of these men of valor ought to serve as incentive and inspiration to preserve that which they created.

SAMUEL ADAMS (1722–1803)

A political activist and patriot without peer, Adams was one of the leading architects of the American Revolution. With remarkable singleness of purpose, this cousin of John Adams devoted himself to the cause of independence, largely neglecting his own interests. In articles and speeches he denounced British tyranny, and he led his patriotic followers to such political acts as the Boston Tea Party. The first to question the British right to tax the colonies, he dared to be identified as a rebel leader—and he was the one, along with John Hancock, that British troops were after when they came to Lexington on April 19, 1775. In 1765 Adams openly encouraged citizens to defy the Stamp Act, and he was the prime mover behind the meeting of all the colonies at the Stamp Act Congress in New York. Adams worked against the British as a member of the Massachusetts legislature, in the powerful position of clerk, and less openly as founder of the Massachusetts committee of correspondence and a leader of the secret society, the Sons of Liberty. This patriotic—and radical—group resorted to violence and demonstrations on several occasions, storming the governor's home and hanging the British tax collector in effigy. On March 5, 1770, a group of colonists threatened British soldiers in Boston, precipitating an incident in which three colonists were killed. Adams and Joseph Warren called it the Boston "Massacre," and news of the "massacre" helped promote anti-British feeling. Adams helped create another incident in December 1773, when the Sons of Liberty, encouraged by Adams, boarded British ships and dumped hundreds of chests of tea overboard—to protest the tax on tea. Adams had a genius for the daring act that would strike political flint. Adams attended the First Continental Congress in 1774, and, on April 18, 1775, he was with Hancock in Lexington, about to go to the Second Congress, when Paul Revere arrived with news that British troops were after them—and they rode off early the next day before the troops arrived, and those first shots were fired. Although he remained active in politics to the end of his life—even serving as the governor of his state—signing the Declaration of Independence was the apex of his career. In his search for freedom and independence Adams was ever impatient, but thanks to his abiding Christian faith, he had the will and the ability to shape events that helped make independence in America a reality in his own time.

CHARLES CARROLL (1737–1832)

One of the largest landholders in America, Charles Carroll was a leader of the Catholic community in Maryland and the only Catholic to sign the Declaration of Independence. Like Washington and Hancock, he risked a great fortune by defying the mother country. After years of study in Europe, Carroll returned to a country indignant over new British taxation, especially the Stamp Act. Although as a Catholic he was unable to hold office, he became a leader of the opposition—partly through newspaper articles he wrote under a pen name. He was a member of the colony's committee of observation, a group directing activities of patriots; the provincial committee of correspondence; and Maryland's unofficial legislature. He actively supported the policy of nonimportation of British goods. In 1776 Congress appointed Carroll, his cousin John, Samuel Chase, and Benjamin Franklin commissioners to Canada—to try to bring Canada into the struggle on the side of the colonies. However, American troops had already invaded Canada, turning the French-Canadians against the American cause. The mission failed. Carroll returned from Canada in June 1776, in time to take a firm stand for independence in the Maryland legislature, and after helping win the legislature's approval, he was selected as a delegate to the Continental Congress, where he signed the Declaration of Independence. For the next twenty-five years, Carroll played a prominent part in both state and national affairs. In Congress during the war, he served with the Board of War and other important committees. A champion of freedom of religion, Carroll contributed to the Maryland Constitution, and though he declined to attend the Constitutional Convention, he supported the new national Constitution. As one of Maryland's senators in the First Congress under that new form of government, he was instrumental in bringing Rhode Island, which had not yet ratified the Constitution, into the Union, and he assisted in drafting the amendments to the Constitution known as the Bill of Rights, finally assuring the freedom of worship and other freedoms for which he had risked so much. When Carroll died in 1832 he was reputed to be the wealthiest man in America—and the last surviving signer of the Declaration of Independence.

SAMUEL CHASE (1741–1811)

Like Samuel Adams and Patrick Henry, Chase was a firebrand political activist. His daring speeches against British tyranny stirred fellow Marylanders as well as members of the Continental Congress to support the cause of independence. Of powerful build and persuasive manner, Chase won a position of leadership in the Maryland colonial legislature while in his twenties. He vigorously opposed the Stamp Act and helped establish the patriotic committee of correspondence in Maryland. At the Continental Congress he was one of the first to speak out for independence. Early in 1776 he went to Canada as a congressional commissioner—with Benjamin Franklin, and John and Charles Carroll—to try to persuade the French-Canadians to join in fighting the British, but the mission was unsuccessful. Chase returned to Philadelphia in time to learn of Richard Lee's resolution on independence, introduced on June 7, but at that time the Maryland delegates were not authorized to vote for independence. Chase left Philadelphia and made a special trip through Maryland to win the people's support, and before the end of June the Maryland convention voted for independence—and its delegates in Philadelphia were authorized to sign the Declaration of Independence. After the war Chase was against the idea of a national government and refused to attend the Constitutional Convention, but by 1790 he was identified with the Federalist Party, and President Washington appointed him to the Supreme Court. As an associate justice, Chase became known for his positive, often impressive opinions, some of which provided an enduring base for the new judicial system. But he was on occasion too much the loyal Federalist: he strongly supported the sedition laws, passed during the Adams administration, which prohibited political opposition to the government, and which Jefferson and his fellow Democrat-Republicans saw as an abridgment of the First Amendment. In 1804, after Chase had uttered some exceedingly intemperate remarks, the House of Representatives initiated impeachment action, but the Senate did not find him guilty. He remained in office, although he was in later years overshadowed by the new chief justice, John Marshall. But he had already made a substantial contribution to the judicial system—and gained the dubious distinction of being the only Founding Father to undergo impeachment proceedings.

GEORGE CLYMER (1739–1813)

The heir of a substantial Philadelphia business and banking fortune, Clymer risked everything to become a leader of the patriots early in the conflict with the king, served in public office for more than twenty years, and signed both the Declaration of Independence and the Constitution. A man of unusual intellectual curiosity, he also served as an officer of the Philadelphia Academy of Fine Arts and the Philadelphia Agricultural Society. One of the first members of Pennsylvania's committee of safety, and one of the first to advocate complete independence from Britain, Clymer was called upon by the Continental Congress to serve as the first treasurer for the United Colonies, and he undertook the almost impossible assignment of raising money to support the government's operations, chief of which was the new Continental Army. And Clymer devoted not only his great energy, but also his own fortune to the cause, exchanging all his money, which was in hard coin, for the shaky continental currency. In late 1776, when Congress fled a threatened Philadelphia, Clymer was one of the committee of three left behind to maintain essential government activities. During this crisis Clymer drove himself almost to a state of exhaustion. Shortly after this ordeal, the British captured Philadelphia and plundered and destroyed his home. In Congress, Clymer performed valuable services as a member of committees dealing with financial matters. During the final years of the war, he was again responsible for obtaining funds for the army. At the Constitutional Convention, Clymer, who was not an exceptional speaker, distinguished himself by his work in committees dealing with his specialty—finance. In 1791, after a term in the First Congress, Clymer served as federal collector of the controversial tax on liquor that led to the Whiskey Rebellion. He concluded his career by negotiating an equitable peace treaty between the United States and the Creek tribe in Georgia. Clymer served the cause from the beginnings of the movement for independence, although he never sought a public office in his life.

JOHN DICKINSON (1732–1808)

Widely known as the "Penman of the Revolution," Dickinson wrote many of the most influential documents of the period—from the *Declaration of Rights* in 1765 and the Articles of Confederation in 1776 to the *Fabius Letter* in 1787, which helped win over the first states to ratify the Constitution—Delaware and Pennsylvania. Having studied law in England, Dickinson was devoted to the English common law system, and his writings before 1776 aimed to correct the misuse of power and preserve the union of the colonies and Britain. His most famous writings were *Letters from a Farmer in Pennsylvania,* which condemned the Townshend Acts and were widely read throughout the colonies; *Petition to the King,* which was a statement of grievances and an appeal for justice, with a pledge of loyalty adopted by Congress; and *Declaration on the Causes and Necessity of Taking up Arms.* This last document— which Congress also adopted, defended the colonies' use of arms for "the preservation of our liberties," and stated that the colonists were simply fighting to regain the liberty that was theirs as Englishmen. In the Continental Congress, Dickinson opposed the idea of declaring independence at first, but, once it was done, he supported the cause and prepared a draft of the Articles of Confederation. Although over forty, Dickinson enlisted in the militia and saw action in New Jersey and Pennsylvania. He returned to Congress in 1779, in time to sign the Articles of Confederation. Because Delaware and Pennsylvania were under a single proprietor, a citizen could hold office in either one, and Dickinson served as president of first Delaware and then Pennsylvania. He played the important role of conciliator at the Constitutional Convention: he saw the need for a stable national government, and he joined Roger Sherman of Connecticut in supporting the idea of two legislative bodies—one with proportional, one with equal representation—the Great Compromise that broke the deadlock between the large and small states.

After the Constitution was sent to the states, Dickinson published a series of letters that explained and defended the Constitution, and that helped win the first ratifications. The penman had done his work well: Jefferson called him "one of the great worthies of the Revolution."

BENJAMIN FRANKLIN (1706–90)

Patriot, inventor, scientist, philosopher, musician, editor, printer, and diplomat, Benjamin Franklin brought the prestige of his unparalleled achievements to the public service that consumed more than half of his life. He was the living example of the richness of life that man can achieve with the freedom—and the will—to do so. In many senses, he was the first American, and he was a Founding Father of the first rank. His rise from apprentice to man of affairs was paralleled by an ever-widening circle of interests. His curiosity led him from subject to subject: he mastered printing, learned French, invented a stove, discovered electrical principles, organized a postal service, and helped discover the Gulf Stream. Although a freethinker—an oddity among his overwhelmingly devout Christian peers—he was the close friend and publisher of George Whitefield, the great evangelist. As his country's representative in England in the 1760s, he defended America's position before hostile, arrogant officials; he helped win repeal of the Stamp Act and pleaded for American representation in Parliament. In the 1770s he continued to try to reason with British officials, but they were inflexible. He returned to America, ready to support the cause of independence. In the Continental Congress, Franklin headed the committee that organized the American postal system, helped draft the Articles of Confederation, and began negotiations with the French for aid. And he helped draft and signed the Declaration of Independence. Franklin was the colonies' best choice as commissioner to France: well known as a scientist and philosopher, he was warmly welcomed in Paris, and his position as a world figure, coupled with his diplomatic skill, helped him negotiate the alliance with France (1778), which brought America desperately needed military support. Soon after, he began negotiating with the British for peace, but only after the French fleet had joined with Washington to defeat Cornwallis at Yorktown would the British consider granting independence. Franklin signed the peace treaty September 3, 1783. After he returned to America, Franklin had one more vital role to play: at the Constitutional Convention his very presence gave weight and authority to the proceedings, and he used his influence to moderate conflicts. On the final day he appealed to the delegates: "I confess that there are several parts of this Constitution which I do not at present approve, but I am not sure I shall never approve them. For having lived long, I have experienced many instances of being obliged by better information, or fuller consideration, to change opinions even on important subjects, which I once thought right, but found to be otherwise. I cannot help expressing a wish that every member of the Convention who may still have objections to it, would with me, on this occasion, doubt a little of his own infallibility, and to make manifest our unanimity, put his name on this instrument." A few minutes later all but three delegates signed the Constitution.

ELBRIDGE GERRY (1744–1814)

A patriot who signed the Declaration of Independence and the Articles of Confederation but refused to sign the Constitution, Elbridge Gerry worked vigorously for independence from the "prostituted government of Great Britain" yet feared the dangers of "too much democracy." At the Constitutional Convention, Gerry refused to sign the Constitution because he could not accept the proposed division of powers or the absence of a Bill of Rights. Although he championed the people and their rights, he believed that the common man could be too easily swayed by unprincipled politicians for democracy to work. But he was not altogether consistent, for he was also jealous of power, fearful of possible tyranny. Devoted to the patriots' cause in the early 1770s, Gerry was active as a member of the Massachusetts committee of correspondence and the first Provincial Congress. As one of the Congress's committee of safety, he was almost captured by British troops the night before the battles of Lexington and Concord. In the Continental Congress he supported the Articles of Confederation—with equal representation for all states, large and small. Gerry represented his district in the first session of the Congress, but he refused to run after two terms. However, he was called to further service when, in 1797, President Adams selected him as a commissioner to France, along with John Marshall and Charles Pinckney, to attempt to improve American relations with the revolutionary French government. French agents—identified as X, Y, and Z—insulted the commissioners by seeking bribes, and Marshall and Pinckney left. Gerry stayed and tried to negotiate with Talleyrand—albeit, unsuccessfully. Upon his return, Gerry claimed credit for reducing the tensions between France and America. As governor of Massachusetts, in 1812 Gerry approved an unusual redistricting that favored his Democratic-Republican Party; one of the more extreme districts, shaped something like a salamander, was depicted by a cartoonist as a beast labeled "Gerrymander"—a term that has become a part of America's political language. Gerry was elected vice president when Madison was elected to a second term in 1812, and was serving in his official capacity when he died suddenly. Ironically, he was riding to the Capitol to perform the duties of president of the Senate, a constitutional function of the vice president that he had objected to in 1787, and one of the reasons he had refused to sign the U.S. Constitution.

ALEXANDER HAMILTON (1755–1804)

Washington's most valued assistant in war and peace, Hamilton was probably the most brilliant writer, organizer, and political theorist among the Founding Fathers. Time after time from 1776 to 1795 he brought his great powers of intellect to bear on the most critical problems facing the new nation—from obtaining a truly national constitution to establishing a sound national financial system. Born in the British West Indies, he came to America as a teenager. William Livingston of New Jersey, who later joined Hamilton in signing the Constitution, gave the talented young man a home and sent him to college. By 1775 Hamilton had written two pamphlets defending the American cause that displayed an exceptional grasp of the principles of government. During the war Hamilton distinguished himself in battle and served as Washington's aide. He organized Washington's headquarters and wrote many of Washington's statements and a complete set of military regulations. An advocate of a strong central government, Hamilton led the delegates at the inconclusive Annapolis convention to agree to meet in Philadelphia the next year "to take into consideration the situation of the United States, . . . to render the Constitution of the Federal Government adequate to the exigencies of the Union." His carefully worded proposal permitted more than it seemed to say: he opened the way for the Constitutional Convention. His influence was not so great at the Convention as after it, when he wrote fifty of the eighty-five Federalist Papers, which won necessary public support. As first secretary of the treasury, Hamilton devised a comprehensive financial system that proved almost immediately successful: he proposed that the federal government assume the states' war debts, and, to settle these and foreign debts, that there be an excise tax, a national bank, and a protective tariff, which would also encourage American industry. The businessmen favored by these measures gradually grew into a political party under Hamilton. As first leader of the Federalist Party, Hamilton was, with Jefferson—who founded the Democratic-Republican Party—a founder of the two-party system. Hamilton, who had little faith in the people, stood for an industrial society, a strong national government, and an aristocracy of power; Jefferson for an agricultural society, strong state government, and political democracy. Jefferson was more concerned with individual rights and freedom, Hamilton with governmental systems and procedures. Rivalry between the factions came to a head when Hamilton was killed in a duel by his New York rival, Aaron Burr. The Constitution and the Federalist Papers, the national financial system and the American two-party system—in a very real sense these are the legacy of the brilliant man who came to America a penniless youth.

BENJAMIN HARRISON (1726–91)

A wealthy Virginia planter and political leader, Harrison risked his vast holdings along the James River by embracing the cause of independence from the time of the Stamp Act through the Revolution—and suffered severe losses during the war when British troops plundered his property. While serving in the Virginia legislature, Harrison helped draft an official protest against the Stamp Act, and his activities as a member of the committee of correspondence and of the First Provincial Congress led to his selection as a delegate to the Continental Congress. There he served on three important committees, dealing with foreign affairs, the army, and the navy—the working committees that formed the nucleus of what later became major departments of the federal government. Harrison also served in Congress as chairman of the committee of the whole, and, on July 2, 1776, he presided over the discussions that led to the vote in favor of Richard Lee's resolution for independence. Harrison's signature on the Declaration of Independence is next to that of his fellow Virginian, Thomas Jefferson. In the Congress, Harrison also presided over the debates that led to the adoption of the Articles of Confederation. During the war Harrison served as speaker of the Virginia legislature and as governor, the position he held when the British surrendered at Yorktown. During his tenure in that latter office, Virginia ceded to the federal government her claim to the lands north and west of the Ohio River, an action in which Jefferson played a major role, and one that helped strengthen the new Union. As a member of the Virginia convention that met to consider ratifying the Constitution, Harrison was chairman of the committee on elections, but he did not participate in many debates. He did, however, join

Patrick Henry in refusing to support the Constitution without a Bill of Rights. Of all the Founding Fathers, Harrison is the only one who has the distinction of having two direct descendants—a son and a great-grandson—who served as president of the United States: William Henry Harrison, the ninth president under the current Constitution and Benjamin Harrison, the twenty-third under the current Constitution.

PATRICK HENRY (1736–99)

The most famous orator of the Revolution, Henry delivered dramatic speeches that kindled the spark of liberty in colonial Virginians and was, according to Thomas Jefferson, "far above all in maintaining the spirit of the Revolution." In 1765, before the House of Burgesses, Henry spoke out boldly against the Stamp Act, firing the colony's opposition, and, in 1775, just weeks before Lexington and Concord, he closed a stirring appeal to arm the militia with the immortal phrase, "Give me liberty, or give me death!" A failure as a farmer and storekeeper, Henry studied law and quickly won a reputation as a lawyer. In 1763, in the "Parson's Cause" case, he gained fame throughout Virginia by winning a point of law against the king's nullification of a Virginia law. In the House of Burgesses in 1765, he responded to news of the Stamp Act by offering five daring resolutions that declared the colonists' rights, including the exclusive right to tax themselves, and he sought support with a fiery speech that evoked cries of "Treason." But Henry's powerful words helped stiffen resistance to the Stamp Act throughout the colonies and added to his reputation. In Virginia, he had more real power than the governor. At the First Continental Congress, Henry strongly supported the Continental Association, a union of colonies for the purpose of boycotting British imports. It was at Virginia's revolutionary convention at Richmond that Henry, after proposing immediate arming of the militia, delivered the most famous speech of the Revolution, concluding, "Gentlemen may cry, peace, peace!—but there is no peace. The war is actually begun! . . . Is life so dear, or peace so sweet, as to be purchased at the price of chains and slavery? Forbid it, Almighty God! I know not what course others may take, but as for me: Give me liberty, or give me death!" The Convention promptly approved his proposal, crying out, "To arms! To arms!" In the Continental Congress in 1775, Henry favored the idea of a Continental Army. No soldier himself, Henry resigned a commission after a short time. As a member of the Virginia patriotic convention, he helped draft the state's constitution and Bill of Rights. He became Virginia's first governor on July 5, 1776, and held the position for the legal limit of three years. Although a leader of the Revolution, Henry was first and foremost a Virginian—when the Constitution came to Virginia for ratification, he fought it, believing it placed too much power in the federal government, depriving the states and the people of essential rights. And his fight against the Constitution and for the Bill of Rights, brought that issue to public notice throughout the colonies—contributing to the early adoption of the Bill of Rights amendments.

WILLIAM JOHNSON (1727–1819)

The only Founding Father who in 1776 was not in favor of independence, Johnson grew into a strong supporter of the new nation: he helped draft the Constitution, signed it, and stoutly defended it at the Connecticut Ratification Convention. Although he attended the Stamp Act Congress in 1765 and served as a special agent for Connecticut in England, Johnson during these years was firmly convinced that the colonies and Great Britain would settle their differences. His stay in London, where he associated with Dr. Samuel Johnson, the great critic and lexicographer, and other notables, undoubtedly strengthened his ties with England, although in London he worked closely with Benjamin Franklin, then agent for Pennsylvania and other colonies, in representing colonial interests. And he supported the American policy of nonimportation of British goods as a protest against the Townshend Acts. After returning, Johnson was elected to serve in the First Continental Congress, but since he was against the idea of independence, he declined the position. Still devoted to the idea of a peaceful settlement, in 1775 he visited the British commander, Gen. Thomas Gage, in Boston—sent by the Connecticut legislature. His mission was unsuccessful, and he was for a time held by patriots there. He resigned from the Connecticut legislature, and from 1777 to 1779 his refusal to support independence cost him his law practice—which the state permitted him to resume after he swore allegiance to Connecticut. Despite his tardy adoption of the cause of independence, Johnson was an influential member of the Congress of Confederation. At the Constitutional Convention, Johnson, a soft-spoken but effective speaker, helped defend and explain the "Connecticut Compromise," the proposal for representing the states in the Senate and the people in the House of Representatives that was finally adopted—to settle the dispute between the large and small states. The scholarly Johnson, who was one of the colonies' leading classicists and who was then serving as president of Columbia College, was chairman of the committee on style that produced the final version of the Constitution—although Gouverneur Morris wrote most of it. He eloquently defended the Constitution at the Connecticut Ratification Convention, and, after ratification, his state selected him to serve as one of the men to sit in the newly formed Senate.

RUFUS KING (1755–1827)

For more than forty years King served his country as a state legislator, member of Congress, delegate to the Constitutional Convention, senator, minister to Great Britain, and candidate for vice president, and president. He helped draft both the Northwest Ordinance and the Constitution, which he signed and later supported at the Massachusetts Ratification Convention. A student during most of the war, King began his public service as a member of the Massachusetts legislature, where he demonstrated his interest in the national cause by championing a bill that provided for regular financial support to the Congress of the Confederation. Later, while serving in Congress, he joined with Jefferson in contributing an antislavery provision to the Northwest Ordinance, the document that prescribed the conditions for the formation of new states from the Northwest Territory. At the Constitutional Convention, where he was recognized as one of the most eloquent speakers, King maintained his position against slavery and supported the idea of a national government with clear authority beyond that of the states. As a member of the first Senate, the Federalist King supported the policies and programs of Washington's administration. He backed Hamilton's financial plans and served as a director of the Bank of the United States, which he helped establish. In 1796 he resigned from the Senate to become minister to Great Britain, a position that taxed his considerable diplomatic ability—helping to keep America neutral while France and Britain were at war. In the elections of 1804 and 1808, King was a vice presidential candidate, running both times on the unsuccessful Federalist ticket with Charles Cotesworth Pinckney of South Carolina. In 1816 King was himself the Federalist candidate for president, losing to James Monroe. But King continued to serve in the Senate, where in 1820 he opposed the Missouri Compromise—with the admission of Missouri as a slave state—as a failure to deal squarely with the problem of slavery. Forcefully but unsuccessfully, he advocated the abolition of slavery. Handsome and sociable, King achieved success as a legislator and diplomat, and he won high praise as a speaker from one of America's most celebrated speakers. Of King, Daniel Webster wrote: "You never heard such a speaker. In strength, and dignity, and fire; in ease, in natural effect, and gesture as well as in matter, he is unequaled."

JOHN MARSHALL (1755–1835)

Unique among the Founding Fathers, Marshall was a young officer in the Continental Army who played only a minor role in the Revolution. In addition, he did not contribute to, or sign, either the Declaration of Independence or the Constitution, but, as chief justice of the Supreme Court, he did more than any other man to institutionalize the new national government by establishing the authority of the Court as coequal with the legislative and executive branches, and by clarifying the fundamental relationship between the states and the national government. Contributions of such magnitude place John Marshall among the first rank of the nation's founders. Although Marshall was only a junior officer in the Revolution—he fought at Brandywine, Germantown, and Monmouth, and endured Valley Forge—his experience in the war led him to see the need for a strong national government, for he believed that a stronger, better-organized government might have more effectively managed the limited resources available to the colonies to wage war. In addition, his military service provided the kind of experience that permitted him to think in *national* terms. Raised in the near wilderness of the frontier, Marshall was thrust into the world of the Continental Army as a teenager. Later he acknowledged that he became an American before he had had a chance to become a Virginian. In the 1790s Marshall was well established as a leader of the Federalists in Virginia. He declined President Washington's offer of the position of attorney general; he publicly defended the Jay Treaty; and in 1797 he was appointed by President Adams as a commissioner to France—for what became known as the XYZ Affair. When Marshall was appointed chief justice, the Supreme Court stood far below the executive and legislative branches in power and prestige. By sheer force of intellect he produced decisions that won wide approval from constitutional lawyers, associates on the Court, and eventually American citizens in general. He was so successful, so inevitably right in many of his views, that he *made* the Court the recognized interpreter of the Constitution. From 1801 to 1835 he delivered the opinion in more than five hundred cases, twenty-five of which were fundamental constitutional questions. Marshall's influence on our system was so great that the Constitution as we know it is, in large measure, Marshall's interpretation of it. A century and a half later, Marshall is still considered foremost of constitutional lawyers. According to a contemporary, Judge Jeremiah Mason, without Marshall's monumental efforts the government of the new nation "would have fallen to pieces."

GEORGE MASON (1725–92)

Thomas Jefferson called him "the wisest man of his generation." Although he signed neither the Declaration of Independence nor the Constitution, Mason was the source of some of the most revolutionary ideas in both of those documents. The drafters of both drew ideas from documents that were largely his—the Virginia Declaration of Rights and the Virginia Constitution. A Southern aristocrat with a five-thousand-acre plantation, which he managed himself, Mason was a neighbor and friend of Washington. As a member of the House of Burgesses in 1769, Mason prepared resolutions against the importing of British goods, which Washington presented and the legislature adopted. In 1774 Mason wrote the Fairfax Resolves, advocating that all of the colonies meet in Congress and that Virginia cease all relations with Britain. He was also primarily responsible for Virginia's relinquishing its claim to the lands beyond the Ohio River, the Northwest Territory, and he influenced Jefferson in his drafting of the Northwest Ordinance, with its prohibition of slavery and its provision for the formation of new states. This Virginia planter played an unusual role at the Constitutional Convention, for he hated slavery, which he called "diabolical in itself and disgraceful to mankind," and he urged delegates at the Convention to give the new government the power to prevent the expansion of slavery. When the Constitution was completed, he refused to sign, partly because he felt the Constitution failed to deal strongly enough with the institution of slavery, permitting the importing of slaves until 1808, partly because it gave the Senate and president too much power and provided no protective bill of rights. He continued his opposition at the Virginia Ratification Convention, joining Patrick Henry, Benjamin Harrison, Richard Henry Lee, and others who feared too powerful a central government. But Mason lived to see his most cherished ideas of the rights of the individual incorporated into the Constitution as the Bill of Rights amendments in December 1791.

A rationalist who had little faith in the workings of governmental bodies, Mason fought passionately for the freedom of the individual—citizen or slave; and he was largely responsible for ensuring that protection of the rights of the individual would be such an essential part of the American system.

GOUVERNEUR MORRIS (1752–1816)

His words are among the most recognizable of any of the Founding Fathers: "We, the people of the United States, in order to form a more perfect union, establish justice, insure domestic tranquility." Morris, who was primarily responsible for the final draft of the Constitution, was also an eloquent, although sometimes windy, speaker, and members of the New York legislature, the Constitutional Convention, and the Senate were often swayed by his masterful blend of logic, wit, and imagination. Although he had strong aristocratic tendencies, and as late as 1774 wrote, "It is in the interest of all men to seek for reunion with the parent state," in 1776 Morris spoke in the New York legislature on behalf of the colonies and against the king. He early recognized the need for a united, strong national congress. Of Morris, historian David Muzzey wrote, "He was a nationalist before the birth of the nation."

In the Continental Congress, Morris was chairman of several committees and his gifted pen produced such important documents as the instructions to Franklin as minister to France, and detailed instructions to the peace commissioners, which contained provisions that ultimately appeared in the final treaty. As a member of Congress, he supported and signed the Articles of Confederation. At the Constitutional Convention, Morris participated in debates more than any other delegate. He argued that the president and the Senate should be elected for life, and that the Senate should represent the rich and propertied, to counterbalance the democratic character of the House of Representatives. This was, of course, rejected, but his proposal for a Council of State led to the idea of the president's cabinet, and he proposed that the president be elected, not by Congress, but by the people. When the Constitution was completed, Morris was given the task of editing and revising it, and he then wrote the famous words of the preamble. Once the Constitution was formally accepted, Morris proved one of its most devoted supporters. On September 17, the day the delegates signed it, Morris made an impassioned speech answering Edmund Randolph, who refused to sign. As minister to France in the 1790s, Morris found himself in the wrong country at the wrong time. Although he was recognized by the French revolutionists as one of the leaders of the American Revolution, he was nonetheless a Federalist with clear aristocratic sympathies. In Paris he became involved in attempts to help French nobles escape—including the Marquis de Lafayette and the king, and the revolutionists demanded his removal. After he returned he served in the Senate and, later, as chairman of the group that developed the plan for the Erie Canal, the waterway that opened the path for westward expansion.

ROBERT MORRIS (1734–1806)

A Philadelphia merchant of great wealth who became the "financier of the Revolution," Morris frequently risked his fortune on behalf of the Continental Army—and in the end, did indeed lose everything. With Roger Sherman, Morris shares the distinction of having signed all three of the principal founding documents—the Declaration of Independence, the Articles of Confederation, and the Constitution. A conservative among the patriots, Morris did little besides sign a protest against the Stamp Act before he was elected to Congress in 1775, and he did not originally support the idea of independence, believing that the time was not ripe. He did, however, sign the Declaration—after he had abstained from the vote. And, in 1778, he signed the Articles of Confederation. In 1776, as chairman of the executive committee of Congress, Morris was left in charge of the government when Congress fled Philadelphia, then threatened by the British. Later that year Washington requested funds for an offensive, and Morris, pledging his personal credit, obtained the money that enabled Washington to defeat the Hessians at Trenton in December. For the remainder of the war, Morris was, either officially or unofficially, the chief civilian in charge of finance and supply. In May 1781 Congress appointed him to the new position of Superintendent of Finance, and that summer he worked closely with Washington in planning the support for the major offensive against Cornwallis at Yorktown. Again Morris backed the purchase of ammunition and supplies with his personal pledge. After the war Morris continued as principal finance officer for Congress, caught between the obligations of the Confederation and the states' continued refusal to support it. He all but exhausted his own credit and repeatedly planned to resign, but he stayed on. He established the first national bank, but Pennsylvania challenged its charter. By 1784, when he finally resigned, the United States had practically no credit abroad—and he himself was nearly bankrupt. As a result, he urged the establishment of a stronger national government. At the Annapolis convention he supported the idea of the convention in Philadelphia. Host to

Washington during the Constitutional Convention, Morris nominated Washington to preside and signed the completed document in September. Morris declined Washington's offer of the position of secretary of the treasury in the new government and was elected one of Pennsylvania's first senators. After he returned to private life his debts finally caught up to him. From 1798 to 1801 he was incarcerated in Philadelphia's debtor's prison. He came out a broken and forgotten man.

CHARLES PINCKNEY (1757–1824)

The "Pinckney Plan" was one of the three plans offered to the Constitutional Convention in Philadelphia. No record of it exists, but Pinckney is generally given credit for many provisions—possibly as many as thirty—of the finished Constitution. In an extremely active career, Pinckney also served four terms as governor of South Carolina, congressman, senator, and minister to Spain. Educated in England, Pinckney returned to assist—and then replace—his father in South Carolina's patriotic movement. Before he was twenty he had served on the state's executive council and helped draft its first constitution. In the war he served with the militia, was captured, and spent a year in a British prison. Elected to the Congress of the Confederation in 1784, Pinckney gradually became convinced of the weakness of the government under the Articles of Confederation. As chairman of a congressional committee considering measures to strengthen the Articles of Confederation, Pinckney gained experience that prepared him for his role at the Constitutional Convention. In 1786, in an address to Congress, he urged that a general convention be called to revise the Articles of Confederation. When Pinckney arrived at the Constitutional Convention in Philadelphia in May 1787, he had already prepared his "Plan." Unfortunately he presented it to the Convention immediately after Edmund Randolph completed a three-hour description of his own plan, and Pinckney's was never debated point by point, but simply referred, with other plans, to the committee on detail. And that committee did not identify, in its comprehensive report, the source of each recommended element of the Constitution. Although the exact extent of Pinckney's contribution to the Constitution remains unknown, Pinckney in later life made such extravagant claims that he became known as "Constitution Charlie." Pinckney also prepared a large part of South Carolina's new constitution, adopted in 1790—a document modeled after the national Constitution. For more than thirty years after the Constitution was ratified, Pinckney served in public office. In the 1790s he left the Federalist Party to support Jefferson. In 1795 he denounced the Jay Treaty, and in the 1800 election, he helped Jefferson carry South Carolina, even though his cousin, Charles Cotesworth Pinckney, was the vice presidential candidate on the Federalist ticket. President Jefferson's appointment of Pinckney as minister to Spain looked very much like a reward, but Pinckney had little success in dealing with Spain. After his return he continued to be elected to public office, completing his career in the Congress, where one of his final acts was to oppose the Missouri Compromise.

CHARLES COTESWORTH PINCKNEY (1746–1825)

"If I had a vein that did not beat with the love of my country, I myself would open it." Such were the sentiments of this Southern patriot who, although educated in England, was one of the principal Southern leaders of the new nation. Charles Cotesworth Pinckney was twice the unsuccessful Federalist candidate for president—in 1804 against Jefferson and in 1808 against Madison—but he is remembered primarily as a courageous army officer, a signer of the Constitution, and as the commissioner to France who, in 1798, refused a veiled request for bribes with, "Millions for defense but not one cent for tribute." After studying law under William Blackstone at Oxford, Pinckney attended the Royal Military Academy in France, gaining training that helped him, after he returned to America, to win a commission as a captain in the Continental Army in 1775. He fought in several battles and was captured when the British took Charleston in 1780. By the end of the war he was a brigadier general. Even before the war Pinckney was active in the patriotic movement. In 1775 he was a member of a group responsible for the local defense, and in February 1776 he was chairman of a committee that drafted a plan for the temporary government of South Carolina. At the Constitutional Convention, Pinckney stoutly defended

Southern interests and states' rights; he revealed little faith in elections by the people, but he accepted the decisions of the convention, signed the Constitution, and supported it at the South Carolina Ratification Convention. One of the most successful lawyers in South Carolina, Pinckney was offered a seat on the Supreme Court by Washington, but he declined—as he did later offers by Washington of the positions of secretary of war and secretary of state. However, in 1796 he accepted the position of minister to France, but, after he arrived in Paris, the French Directory chose not to accept him, and he went to Holland. In 1797 President Adams appointed Pinckney, John Marshall, and Elbridge Gerry commissioners to France—to attempt to settle differences, but the three were insulted by the French officials known as X, Y, and Z, and Pinckney made his famous reply and returned home something of a hero. He was soon appointed major general in the newly formed army, hastily organized by Washington because of the rupture with France, but by 1800 tensions were reduced. Although he was twice unsuccessful in seeking the presidency, Pinckney was honored by his fellow officers of the Revolution and served from 1805 until his death as president of their association, the Society of the Cincinnati.

EDMUND RANDOLPH (1753–1813)

On May 29, 1787, Randolph introduced the Virginia Plan to the Constitutional Convention—the first time the idea of a new national form of government was formally presented to the delegates at Philadelphia. Although Madison contributed much to the plan, it was the handsome thirty-three-year-old governor of Virginia, spokesman for his state, who began the Convention's serious deliberations by outlining the fifteen resolves that called for a national executive, judiciary, and legislature. It was a dramatic moment: the delegates, officially gathered "for the sole and express purpose of revising the Articles of Confederation," were confronted with a radical proposal to create a completely different governmental system. That they heard Randolph out—for more than three hours—and even considered the plan he offered, testifies to Randolph's success. But he was not pleased with some of the additions and revisions to the Virginia Plan that delegates introduced later, and he several times shifted his position, for and against; in September he refused to sign the final document. However, at the Virginia Ratification Convention, he shocked anti-Federalists like Patrick Henry by reversing himself and supporting the Constitution. Randolph explained his new position—by this time eight states had already ratified the Constitution, only one more was needed, and other states had already urged that Bill of Rights amendments should be enacted soon after ratification, satisfying Randolph's objection to the original Constitution. In a telling speech, Patrick Henry slyly suggested that perhaps there were other reasons—not going as far as mentioning a promised post in the new government, but the hint was enough: the two men came close to fighting a duel. After Washington was elected president, he named Randolph the first attorney general, but Randolph denied that this was in any way related to his supporting the Constitution. As attorney general he established the office and the beginnings of the Justice Department, and after Jefferson resigned as secretary of state, Randolph assumed that position also. In 1795 he was accused of seeking bribes from the French ambassador, and although he proved himself innocent, he resigned and never held another public office.

ROGER SHERMAN (1721–93)

A Yankee cobbler who taught himself law and became a judge and a legislator, Roger Sherman helped draft four of the major American founding documents—the Declaration of Independence, the Articles of Confederation, the Constitution and the Bill of Rights. Sherman had almost twenty years' experience as a colonial legislator behind him when he came to the First Continental Congress in 1774, and he quickly won the respect of his fellow delegates for his wisdom, industry, and sound judgment. John Adams called him "one of the soundest and strongest pillars of the Revolution." In Congress, Sherman was one of the first to deny Parliament's authority to make laws for America, and he strongly supported the boycott of British goods. In the following years he served with Jefferson and Franklin on the committee that drafted the Declaration of Independence, and on the one that drafted the Articles of Confederation. He also served on the maritime committee, the board of treasury and the board of war—all of first importance to the Revolution. A Puritan of simple habits who performed all tasks with thoroughness and accuracy, Sherman gained more legislative experience in his years in Congress than any other member; by the time he left he was perhaps the most powerful—and most overworked—of congressmen. Sherman's greatest contribution—and the best known—was the "Connecticut Compromise" he proposed at the Constitutional Convention: by proposing that Congress have two branches, one with proportional, one with equal representation, he satisfied both the small and the large states, providing a solution to one of the most stubborn problems of the Convention. In Connecticut he defended the Constitution, writing articles in the New Haven *Gazette,* and helped win ratification in January 1788. Connecticut was the fifth state to ratify. Sherman was the oldest man elected to the new national House of Representatives. In the first Congress he served on the committee that prepared and reviewed the Bill of Rights amendments. By coincidence, the year that the Bill of Rights became part of the Constitution, Sherman was elected senator—so that the man who conceived the "Connecticut Compromise" had the opportunity to represent that state in both of the legislative branches that he helped to create.

JAMES WILSON (1742–98)

"The best form of government which has ever been offered to the world," James Wilson called the Constitution, which he helped draft and later signed. He also signed the Declaration of Independence and served as associate justice of the first Supreme Court. Although born and educated in Scotland, Wilson became a leader of the patriots after fleeing the English oppression of his homeland. He studied law under John Dickinson in Philadelphia—and the two served in the Continental Congress together. In 1774, before he was elected to Congress, Wilson wrote a carefully reasoned pamphlet, *Considerations on the Legislative Authority of the British Parliament,* which boldly concluded that Parliament had no authority over the colonies. In Congress he was one of three Pennsylvania members to vote for independence. In a bizarre incident in 1779, Wilson's home was attacked by a faction of patriots who felt Wilson had betrayed the cause by defending in court merchants charged with treason. However, after the war he continued to represent Pennsylvania—in Congress and at the Constitutional Convention. At the Constitutional Convention Wilson had a dual role— as a delegate and as spokesman for the elderly and infirm Benjamin Franklin. As a lawyer and political theorist, Wilson was deeply committed to the principle that sovereignty resides with the people, and he advocated popular elections for both the president and Congress. A member of the committee on detail, he wrote a draft of the Constitution that provided the basis for the final document, and throughout the convention he delivered the persuasive words of Franklin that moved the delegates to overlook minor differences and finally approve the Constitution.

Later, in 1787 at the Pennsylvania Ratification Convention, Wilson delivered a persuasive speech of his own, winning the votes necessary for ratification. Two years later his state called on him to draft a new state constitution. During the first years under the new Constitution, Wilson served on the Supreme Court. In addition, as a lecturer in law at the College of Philadelphia, he undertook to translate the principle of the sovereignty of the people into the realm of law, providing legal justification for the Revolution and the beginnings of a uniquely American system of jurisprudence.

THE CONSTITUTION

On May 25, 1787, a constitutional convention convened in Philadelphia with representatives from seven states. Their purpose was to draft amendments to the Articles of Confederation. Eventually, however, they determined that in order to achieve their ends they would have to create an entirely new document. By September 17, 1787, twelve state delegations had contributed to an acceptable draft of the new document. Requiring the ratification of only nine states to take effect, the document met stiff opposition and failed to become official until June 21, 1788. It would take until May 29, 1790, before all of the thirteen original states would actually ratify.

We the people of the United States, in order to form a more perfect union, establish justice, insure domestic tranquillity, provide for the common defense, promote the general welfare, and secure the blessings of liberty to ourselves and our posterity, do ordain and establish this Constitution for the United States of America.

ARTICLE I

Section 1: All legislative powers herein granted shall be vested in a Congress of the United States, which shall consist of a Senate and House of Representatives.

Section 2: The House of Representatives shall be composed of members chosen every second year by the people of the several states, and the electors in each state shall have the qualifications requisite for electors of the most numerous branch of the state legislature.

No person shall be a representative who shall not have attained to the age of twenty-five years, and been seven years a citizen of the United States, and who shall not, when elected, be an inhabitant of that state in which he shall be chosen.

Representatives and direct taxes shall be apportioned among the several states which may be included within this Union, according to their respective numbers, which shall be determined by adding to the whole number of free persons, including those bound to service for a term of years, and excluding Indians not taxed, three-fifths of all other persons. The actual enumeration shall be made within three years after the first meeting of the Congress of the United States, and within every subsequent term of ten years, in such manner as they shall by law direct. The number of representatives shall not exceed one for every thirty thousand, but each state shall have at least one representative; and until such enumeration shall be made, the state of New Hampshire shall be entitled to choose three, Massachusetts eight, Rhode Island and Providence Plantations one, Connecticut five, New York six, New Jersey four, Pennsylvania eight, Delaware one, Maryland six, Virginia ten, North Carolina five, South Carolina five, and Georgia three.

When vacancies happen in the representation from any state, the executive authority thereof shall issue writs of election to fill such vacancies.

The House of Representatives shall choose their speaker and other officers; and shall have the sole power of impeachment.

Section 3: The Senate of the United States shall be composed of two senators from each state, chosen by the legislature thereof, for six years; and each senator shall have one vote.

Immediately after they shall be assembled in consequence of the first election, they shall be divided as equally as may be into three classes. The seats of the senators of the first class shall be vacated at the expiration of the second year, of the second class at the expiration of the fourth year, and of the third class at the expiration of the sixth year, so that one third may be chosen every second year; and if vacancies happen by resignation, or otherwise, during the recess of the legislature of any state, the executive thereof may make temporary appointments until the next meeting of the legislature, which shall then fill such vacancies.

No person shall be a senator who shall not have attained to the age of thirty years, and been nine years a citizen of the United States, and who shall not, when elected, be an inhabitant of that state for which he shall be chosen.

The vice president of the United States shall be president of the Senate, but shall have no vote, unless they be equally divided.

The Senate shall choose their other officers, and also a president pro tempore, in the absence of the vice president, or when he shall exercise the office of president of the United States.

The Senate shall have the sole power to try all impeachments. When sitting for that purpose, they shall be on oath or affirmation. When the president of the United States is tried, the chief justice shall preside: and no person shall be convicted without the concurrence of two-thirds of the members present.

Judgment in cases of impeachment shall not extend further than to removal from office, and disqualification to hold and enjoy any office of honor, trust or profit under the United States: but the party convicted shall nevertheless be liable and subject to indictment, trial, judgment, and punishment, according to law.

Section 4: The times, places, and manner of holding elections for senators and representatives shall be prescribed in each state by the legislature thereof; but the Congress may at any time by law make or alter such regulations, except as to the places of choosing senators.

The Congress shall assemble at least once in every year, and such meeting shall be on the first Monday in December, unless they shall by law appoint a different day.

Section 5: Each House shall be the judge of the elections, returns, and qualifications of its own members, and a majority of each shall constitute a quorum to do business; but a smaller number may adjourn from day to day, and may be authorized to compel the attendance of absent members, in such manner, and under such penalties as each House may provide.

Each House may determine the rules of its proceedings, punish its members for disorderly behavior, and, with the concurrence of two-thirds, expel a member.

Each House shall keep a journal of its proceedings, and from time to time publish the same, excepting such parts as may in their judgment require secrecy; and the yeas and nays of the members of either House on any question shall, at the desire of one-fifth of those present, be entered on the journal.

Neither House, during the session of Congress, shall, without the consent of the other, adjourn for more than three days, nor to any other place than that in which the two Houses shall be sitting.

Section 6: The senators and representatives shall receive a compensation for their services, to be ascertained by law, and paid out of the Treasury of the United States. They shall in all cases, except treason, felony, and breach of the peace, be privileged from arrest during their attendance at the session of their respective Houses, and in going to and returning from the same; and for any speech or debate in either House, they shall not be questioned in any other place.

No senator or representative shall, during the time for which he was elected, be appointed to any civil office under the authority of the United States, which shall have been created, or the emoluments whereof shall have been increased during such time; and no person holding any office under the United States shall be a member of either House during his continuance in office.

Section 7: All bills for raising revenue shall originate in the House of Representatives; but the Senate may propose or concur with amendments as on other bills.

Every bill which shall have passed the House of Representatives and the Senate, shall, before it become a law, be presented to the president of the United States; if he approve he shall sign it, but if not he shall return it, with his objections to that House in which it shall have originated, who shall enter the objections at large on their journal, and proceed to reconsider it. If after such reconsideration two-thirds of that House shall agree to pass the bill, it shall be sent, together with the objections, to the other House, by which it shall likewise be reconsidered, and if approved by two-thirds of that House, it shall become a law. But in all such cases the votes of both Houses shall be determined by yeas and nays, and the names of the persons voting for and against the bill shall be entered on the journal of each House respectively. If any bill shall not be returned by the president within ten days (Sundays excepted) after it shall have been presented to him, the same shall be a law, in like manner as if he had signed it, unless the Congress by their adjournment prevent its return, in which case it shall not be a law.

Every order, resolution, or vote to which the concurrence of the Senate and House of Representatives may be necessary (except on a question of adjournment) shall be presented to the president of the United States; and before the same shall take effect, shall be approved by him, or being disapproved by him, shall be re-passed by two-thirds of the Senate and House of Representatives, according to the rules and limitations prescribed in the case of a bill.

Section 8: The Congress shall have power to lay and collect taxes, duties, imposts, and excises, to pay the debts and provide for the common defense and general welfare of the United States; but all duties, imposts, and excises shall be uniform throughout the United States;

To borrow money on the credit of the United States;

To regulate commerce with foreign nations, and among the several states, and with the Indian tribes;

To establish an uniform rule of naturalization, and uniform laws on the subject of bankruptcies throughout the United States;

To coin money, regulate the value thereof, and of foreign coin, and fix the standard of weights and measures;

To provide for the punishment of counterfeiting the securities and current coin of the United States;

To establish post offices and post roads;

To promote the progress of science and useful arts, by securing for limited times to authors and inventors the exclusive right to their respective writings and discoveries;

To constitute tribunals inferior to the Supreme Court;

To define and punish piracies and felonies committed on the high seas, and offenses against the law of nations;

To declare war, grant letters of marque and reprisal, and make rules concerning captures on land and water;

To raise and support armies, but no appropriation of money to that use shall be for a longer term than two years;

To provide and maintain a navy;

To make rules for the government and regulation of the land and naval forces;

To provide for calling forth the militia to execute the laws of the Union, suppress insurrections, and repel invasions;

To provide for organizing, arming, and disciplining the militia, and for governing such part of them as may be employed in the service of the United States, reserving to the states respectively, the appointment of the officers, and the authority of training the militia according to the discipline prescribed by Congress;

To exercise exclusive legislation in all cases whatsoever, over such district (not exceeding ten miles square) as may, by cession of particular states, and the acceptance of Congress, become the seat of the government of the United States, and to exercise like authority over all places purchased by the consent of the legislature of the state in which the same shall be, for the erection of forts, magazines, arsenals, dockyards, and other needful buildings; and,

To make all laws which shall be necessary and proper for carrying into execution the foregoing powers, and all other powers vested by this Constitution in the government of the United States, or in any department or officer thereof.

Section 9: The migration or importation of such persons as any of the states now existing shall think proper to admit, shall not be prohibited by the Congress prior to the year one thousand eight hundred and eight, but a tax or duty may be imposed on such importation, not exceeding ten dollars for each person.

The privilege of the writ of habeas corpus shall not be suspended, unless when in cases of rebellion or invasion the public safety may require it.

No bill of attainder or ex post facto law shall be passed.

No capitation, or other direct, tax shall be laid, unless in proportion to the census or enumeration herein before directed to be taken.

No tax or duty shall be laid on articles exported from any state.

No preference shall be given by any regulation of commerce or revenue to the ports of one state over those of another; nor shall vessels bound to, or from, one state, be obliged to enter, clear, or pay duties in another.

No money shall be drawn from the Treasury, but in consequence of appropriations made by law; and a regular statement and account of the receipts and expenditures of all public money shall be published from time to time.

No title of nobility shall be granted by the United States: and no person holding any office of profit or trust under them, shall, without the consent of the Congress, accept of any present, emolument, office, or title, of any kind whatever, from any king, prince, or foreign state.

Section 10: No state shall enter into any treaty, alliance, or confederation; grant letters of marque and reprisal; coin money; emit bills of credit; make anything but gold and silver coin a tender in payment of debts; pass any bill of attainder, ex post facto law, or law impairing the obligation of contracts; or grant any title of nobility.

No state shall, without the consent of the Congress, lay any imposts or duties on imports or exports, except what may be absolutely necessary for executing its inspection laws: and the net produce of all duties and imposts, laid by any state on imports or exports, shall be for the use of the Treasury of the United States; and all such laws shall be subject to the revision and control of the Congress.

No state shall, without the consent of Congress, lay any duty of tonnage, keep troops or ships of war in time of peace, enter into any agreement or compact with another state or with a foreign power, or engage in war, unless actually invaded, or in such imminent danger as will not admit of delay.

ARTICLE II

Section 1: The executive power shall be vested in a president of the United States of America. He shall hold his office during the term of four years, and, together with the vice president, chosen for the same term, be elected, as follows.

Each state shall appoint, in such manner as the legislature thereof may direct, a number of electors, equal to the whole number of senators and representatives to which the state may be entitled in the Congress: but no senator or representative, or person holding an office of trust or profit under the United States, shall be appointed an elector.

The electors shall meet in their respective states, and vote by ballot for two persons, of whom one at least shall not be an inhabitant of the same state with themselves. And they shall make a list of all the persons voted for, and of the number of votes for each; which list they shall sign and certify, and transmit sealed to the seat of the government of the United States, directed to the president of the Senate. The president of the Senate shall, in the presence of the Senate and House of Representatives, open all the certificates, and the votes shall then be counted. The person having the greatest number of votes shall be the president, if such number be a majority of the whole number of electors appointed; and if there be more than one who have such majority, and have an equal number of votes, then the House of Representatives shall immediately choose by ballot one of them for president; and if no person have a majority, then from the five highest on the list the said House shall in like manner choose the president. But in choosing the president, the votes shall be taken by states, the representation from each state having one vote; a quorum for this purpose shall consist of a member or members from two-thirds of the states, and a majority of all the states shall be necessary to a choice. In every case, after the choice of the president, the person having the greatest number of votes of the electors shall be the vice president. But if there should remain two or more who have equal votes, the Senate shall choose from them by ballot the vice president.

The Congress may determine the time of choosing the electors, and the day on which they shall give their votes; which day shall be the same throughout the United States.

No person except a natural-born citizen, or a citizen of the United States at the time of the adoption of this Constitution, shall be eligible to the office of president; neither shall any person be eligible to that office who shall not have attained to the age of thirty-five years, and been fourteen years a resident within the United States.

In case of the removal of the president from office, or of his death, resignation, or inability to discharge the powers and duties of the said office, the same shall devolve on the vice president, and the Congress may by law provide for the case of removal, death, resignation, or inability, both of the president and vice president, declaring what officer shall then act as president, and such officer shall act accordingly, until the disability be removed, or a president shall be elected.

The president shall, at stated times, receive for his services, a compensation, which shall neither be increased nor diminished during the period for which he shall have been elected, and he shall not receive within that period any other emolument from the United States, or any of them.

Before he enter on the execution of his office, he shall take the following oath or affirmation: "I do solemnly swear (or affirm) that I will faithfully execute the office of president of the United States, and will to the best of my ability, preserve, protect, and defend the Constitution of the United States."

Section 2: The president shall be commander in chief of the army and navy of the United States, and of the militia of the several states, when called into the actual service of the United States; he may require the opinion, in writing, of the principal officer in each of the executive departments, upon any subject relating to the duties of their respective offices, and he shall have power to grant reprieves and pardons for offenses against the United States, except in cases of impeachment.

He shall have power, by and with the advice and consent of the Senate, to make treaties, provided two-thirds of the senators present concur; and he shall nominate, and by and with the advice and consent of the Senate, shall appoint ambassadors, other public ministers and consuls, judges of the Supreme Court, and all other officers of the United States, whose appointments are not herein otherwise provided for, and which shall be established by law: but the Congress may by law vest the appointment of such inferior officers, as they think proper, in the president alone, in the courts of law, or in the heads of departments.

The president shall have power to fill up all vacancies that may happen during the recess of the Senate, by granting commissions which shall expire at the end of their next session.

Section 3: He shall from time to time give to the Congress information of the state of the Union, and recommend to their consideration such measures as he shall judge necessary and expedient, he may, on extraordinary occasions, convene both Houses, or either of them, and in case of disagreement between them, with respect to the time of adjournment, he may adjourn them to such time as he shall think proper; he shall receive ambassadors and other public ministers; he shall take care that the laws be faithfully executed, and shall commission all the officers of the United States.

Section 4: The president, vice president, and all civil officers of the United States shall be removed from office on impeachment for, and conviction of, treason, bribery, or other high crimes and misdemeanors.

ARTICLE III

Section 1: The judicial power of the United States shall be vested in one Supreme Court, and in such inferior courts as the Congress may from time to time ordain and establish. The judges, both of the supreme and inferior courts, shall hold their offices during good behavior, and shall, at stated times, receive for their services, a compensation, which shall not be diminished during their continuance in office.

Section 2: The judicial power shall extend to all cases, in law and equity, arising under this Constitution, the laws of the United States, and treaties made, or which shall be made, under their authority; to all cases affecting ambassadors, other public ministers and consuls; to all cases of admiralty and maritime jurisdiction; to controversies to which the United States shall be a party; to controversies between two or more states—between a state and citizens of another state—between citizens of different states—between citizens of the same state claiming lands under grants of different states, and between a state, or the citizens thereof, and foreign states, citizens, or subjects.

In all cases affecting ambassadors, other public ministers and consuls, and those in which a state shall be party, the Supreme Court shall have original jurisdiction. In all the other cases before mentioned, the Supreme Court shall have appellate jurisdiction, both as to law and fact, with such exceptions, and under such regulations as the Congress shall make.

The trial of all crimes, except in cases of impeachment, shall be by jury; and such trial shall be held in the state where the said crimes shall have been committed; but when not committed within any state, the trial shall be at such place or places as the Congress may by law have directed.

Section 3: Treason against the United States shall consist only in levying war against them, or in adhering to their enemies, giving them aid and comfort. No person shall be convicted of treason unless on the testimony of two witnesses to the same overt act, or on confession in open court.

The Congress shall have power to declare the punishment of treason, but no attainder of treason shall work corruption of blood, or forfeiture except during the life of the person attainted.

ARTICLE IV

Section 1: Full faith and credit shall be given in each state to the public acts, records, and judicial proceedings of every other state. And the Congress may by general laws prescribe the manner in which such acts, records, and proceedings shall be proved, and the effect thereof.

Section 2: The citizens of each state shall be entitled to all privileges and immunities of citizens in the several states.

A person charged in any state with treason, felony, or other crime, who shall flee from justice, and be found in another state, shall on demand of the executive authority of the state from which he fled, be delivered up, to be removed to the state having jurisdiction of the crime.

No person held to service or labor in one state, under the laws thereof, escaping into another, shall, in consequence of any law or regulation therein, be discharged from such service or labor, but shall be delivered up on claim of the party to whom such service or labor may be due.

Section 3: New states may be admitted by the Congress into this Union; but no new state shall be formed or erected within the jurisdiction of any other state; nor any state be formed by the junction of two or more states, or parts of states, without the consent of the legislatures of the states concerned as well as of the Congress.

The Congress shall have power to dispose of and make all needful rules and regulations respecting the territory or other property belonging to the United States; and nothing in this Constitution shall be so construed as to prejudice any claims of the United States, or of any particular state.

Section 4: The United States shall guarantee to every state in this Union a republican form of government, and shall protect each of them against invasion; and on application of the legislature, or of the executive (when the legislature cannot be convened) against domestic violence.

ARTICLE V

The Congress, whenever two-thirds of both Houses shall deem it necessary, shall propose amendments to this Constitution, or, on the application of the legislatures of two-thirds of the several states, shall call a convention for proposing amendments, which, in either case, shall be valid to all intents and purposes, as part of this Constitution, when ratified by the legislatures of three-fourths of the several states, or by conventions in three-fourths thereof, as the one or the other mode of ratification may be proposed by the Congress; provided that no amendment which may be made prior to the year one thousand eight hundred and eight shall in any manner affect the first and fourth clauses in the ninth section of the first article; and that no state, without its consent, shall be deprived of its equal suffrage in the Senate.

ARTICLE VI

All debts contracted and engagements entered into, before the adoption of this Constitution, shall be as valid against the United States under this Constitution, as under the Confederation.

This Constitution, and the laws of the United States which shall be made in pursuance thereof, and all treaties made, or which shall be made, under the authority of the United States, shall be the supreme law of the land; and the judges in every state shall be bound thereby, anything in the constitution or laws of any state to the contrary notwithstanding.

The senators and representatives before mentioned, and the members of the several state legislatures, and all executive and judicial officers, both of the United States and of the several states, shall be bound by oath or affirmation, to support this Constitution; but no religious test shall ever be required as a qualification to any office or public trust under the United States.

ARTICLE VII

The ratification of the conventions of nine states shall be sufficient for the establishment of this Constitution between the states so ratifying the same.

Done in convention by the unanimous consent of the states present the seventeenth day of September in the year of Our Lord one thousand seven hundred and eighty-seven and of the Independence of the United States of America the twelfth. In witness whereof we have hereunto subscribed our names.

THE BILL OF RIGHTS

Because of the opposition to the adoption of the Constitution by the anti-Federalists, several states proposed amending the document to better protect the states as well as individuals from the incursions of the centralized federal government. Thus these ten new planks were drafted, debated, and eventually adopted. They became the first ten amendments to the Constitution— finally ratified on December 15, 1791.

The conventions of a number of states having at the time of their adopting the Constitution, expressed a desire, in order to prevent misconstruction or abuse of its powers, that further declaratory and restrictive clauses should be added: and as extending the ground of public confidence in the government, will best insure the beneficent ends of its institution.

ARTICLE I

Congress shall make no law respecting an establishment of religion, or prohibiting the free exercise thereof; or abridging the freedom of speech, or of the press; or the right of the people peaceably to assemble, and to petition the government for a redress of grievances.

ARTICLE II

A well-regulated militia, being necessary to the security of a free state, the right of the people to keep and bear arms, shall not be infringed.

ARTICLE III

No soldier shall, in time of peace be quartered in any house, without the consent of the owner, nor in time of war, but in a manner to be prescribed by law.

ARTICLE IV

The right of the people to be secure in their persons, houses, papers, and effects, against unreasonable searches and seizures, shall not be violated, and no warrants shall issue, but upon probable cause, supported by oath or affirmation, and particularly describing the place to be searched, and the persons or things to be seized.

ARTICLE V

No person shall be held to answer for a capital, or otherwise infamous crime, unless on a presentment or indictment of a grand jury, except in cases arising in the land or naval forces, or in the militia, when in actual service in time of war or public danger; nor shall any person be subject for the same offense to be twice put in jeopardy of life or limb; nor shall be compelled in any criminal case to be a witness against himself, nor be deprived of life, liberty, or property, without due process of law; nor shall private property be taken for public use, without just compensation.

ARTICLE VI

In all criminal prosecutions, the accused shall enjoy the right to a speedy and public trial, by an impartial jury of the state and district wherein the crime shall have been committed, which district shall have been previously ascertained by law, and to be informed of the nature and cause of the accusation; to be confronted with the witnesses against him; to have compulsory process for obtaining witnesses in his favor, and to have the assistance of counsel for his defense.

ARTICLE VII

In suits at common law, where the value in controversy shall exceed twenty dollars, the right of trial by jury shall be preserved, and no fact tried by a jury shall be otherwise reexamined in any court of the United States, than according to the rules of the common law.

ARTICLE VIII

Excessive bail shall not be required, nor excessive fines imposed, nor cruel and unusual punishments inflicted.

ARTICLE IX

The enumeration in the Constitution, of certain rights, shall not be construed to deny or disparage others retained by the people.

ARTICLE X

The powers not delegated to the United States by the Constitution, nor prohibited by it to the states, are reserved to the states respectively, or to the people.

AMENDMENTS TO
THE CONSTITUTION

Almost immediately after its founding, the American government found discrepancies or omissions in its constitutional framework. As a result, a series of amendments was proposed. Between 1798 and 1870, five were ratified. The first two rectified omissions in the original charter concerning legal actions and the orderly election of the chief executive. The other three were more dramatic adjustments of the charter wrought as a result of the Civil War and Reconstruction. The Eleventh Amendment was ratified in 1798. Five amendments were added in the nineteenth century: the Twelfth Amendment (1804), the Thirteenth Amendment (1865), the Fourteenth Amendment (1868), the Fifteenth Amendment (1870). The twentieth century has seen more adjustment of the nation's constitutional structure than at any other time in our history. Several of the amendments have radically altered the nature and function of the government. Two of the farthest-reaching amendments—the Sixteenth and Seventeenth Amendments—were ratified in a single year: 1913. Another—the Eighteenth Amendment—was ratified in 1919 only to be repealed by another—the Twenty-first Amendment—which was ratified in 1933. The Nineteenth Amendment, giving the franchise to women, was ratified in 1920. The Twentieth Amendment, regulating the terms of federal officials, was ratified in 1933. The Twenty-second Amendment was ratified in 1951, and the Twenty-third Amendment was ratified ten years later in 1961. The Twenty-fourth Amendment, guaranteeing all citizens civil and voting rights, was ratified in 1964. The Twenty-fifth Amendment, providing for orderly succession in the White House, was ratified in 1967. The Twenty-sixth Amendment, lowering the legal voting age, was ratified in 1971. The Twenty-seventh Amendment has had perhaps the most interesting route to ratification; it was first proposed in 1789 and not ratified until more than two hundred years later—in 1992.

AMENDMENT XI

The Judicial power of the United States shall not be construed to extend to any suit in law or equity, commenced or prosecuted against one of the United States by Citizens of another State, or by Citizens or Subjects of any Foreign State.

AMENDMENT XII

The Electors shall meet in their respective States and vote by ballot for President and Vice President, one of whom, at least, shall not be an inhabitant of the same State with themselves; they shall name in their ballots the person voted for as President, and in distinct ballots the person voted for as Vice-President, and they shall make distinct lists of all persons voted for as President, and of all persons voted for as Vice-President, and of the number of votes for each, which lists they shall sign and certify, and transmit sealed to the seat of the government of the United States, directed to the President of the Senate;—The President of the Senate shall, in the presence of the Senate and House of Representatives, open all the certificates and the votes shall then be counted;—The person having the greatest number of votes for President, shall be the President, if such number be a majority of the whole number of Electors appointed; and if no person have such majority, then from the persons having the highest numbers not exceeding three on the list of those voted for as President, the House of Representatives shall choose immediately, by ballot, the President. But in choosing the President, the votes shall be taken by states, the representation from each state having one vote; a quorum for this purpose shall consist of a member or members from two-thirds of the states, and a majority of all the states shall be necessary to a choice. And if the House of Representatives shall not choose a President whenever the right of choice shall devolve upon them, before the fourth day of March next following, then the Vice-President shall act as President, as in the case of the death or other constitutional disability of the President.—The person having the greatest number of votes as Vice-President, shall be the Vice-President, if such number be a majority of the whole number of Electors appointed, and if no person have a majority, then from the two highest numbers on the list, the Senate shall choose the Vice-President; a quorum for the purpose shall consist of two-thirds of the whole number of senators, and a majority of the whole number shall be necessary to a choice. But no person constitutionally ineligible to the office of President shall be eligible to that of Vice-President of the United States.

AMENDMENT XIII

Section 1: Neither slavery nor involuntary servitude, except as a punishment for crime whereof the party shall have been duly convicted, shall exist within the United States, or any place subject to their jurisdiction.

Section 2: Congress shall have power to enforce this article by appropriate legislation.

AMENDMENT XIV

Section 1: All persons born or naturalized in the United States, and subject to the jurisdiction thereof, are citizens of the United States and of the State wherein they reside. No State shall make or enforce any law which shall abridge the privileges or immunities of citizens of the United States; nor shall any State deprive any person of life, liberty, or property, without due process of law; nor deny to any person within its jurisdiction the equal protection of the laws.

Section 2: Representatives shall be apportioned among the several States according to their respective numbers, counting the whole number of persons in each State, excluding Indians not taxed. But when the right to vote at any election for the choice of electors for President and

Vice-President of the United States, Representatives in Congress, the Executive and Judicial officers of a State, or the members of the Legislature thereof, is denied to any of the male inhabitants of such State, being twenty-one years of age, and citizens of the United States, or in any way abridged, except for participation in rebellion, or other crime, the basis of representation therein shall be reduced in the proportion which the number of such male citizens shall bear to the whole number of male citizens twenty-one years of age in such State.

Section 3: No person shall be a Senator or Representative in Congress, or elector of President and Vice-President, or hold any office, civil or military, under the United States, or under any State, who, having previously taken an oath, as a member of Congress, or as an officer of the United States, or as a member of any State legislature, or as an executive or judicial officer of any State, to support the Constitution of the United States, shall have engaged in insurrection or rebellion against the same, or given aid or comfort to the enemies thereof. But Congress may by a vote of two-thirds of each House, remove such disability.

Section 4: The validity of the public debt of the United States, authorized by law, including debts incurred for payment of pensions and bounties for services in suppressing insurrection or rebellion, shall not be questioned. But neither the United States nor any State shall assume or pay any debt or obligation incurred in aid of insurrection or rebellion against the United States, or any claim for the loss or emancipation of any slave; but all such debts, obligations, and claims shall be held illegal and void.

Section 5: The Congress shall have the power to enforce, by appropriate legislation, the provisions of this article.

AMENDMENT XV

Section 1: The right of citizens of the United States to vote shall not be denied or abridged by the United States or by any State on account of race, color, or previous condition of servitude.

Section 2: The Congress shall have power to enforce this article by appropriate legislation.

AMENDMENT XVI

The Congress shall have power to lay and collect taxes on incomes, from whatever source derived, without apportionment among the several States, and without regard to any census or enumeration.

AMENDMENT XVII

The Senate of the United States shall be composed of two Senators from each State, elected by the people thereof, for six years; and each Senator shall have one vote. The electors in each State shall have the qualifications requisite for electors of the most numerous branch of the State legislatures.

When vacancies happen in the representation of any State in the Senate, the executive authority of such State shall issue writs of election to fill such vacancies: Provided, That the legislature of any State may empower the executive thereof to make temporary appointments until the people fill the vacancies by election as the legislature may direct.

This amendment shall not be so construed as to affect the election or term of any Senator chosen before it becomes valid as part of the Constitution.

AMENDMENT XVIII

Section 1: After one year from the ratification of this article the manufacture, sale, or transportation of intoxicating liquors within, the importation thereof into, or the exportation thereof from the United States and all territory subject to the jurisdiction thereof for beverage purposes is hereby prohibited.

Section 2: The Congress and the several States shall have concurrent power to enforce this article by appropriate legislation.

Section 3: This article shall be inoperative unless it shall have been ratified as an amendment to the Constitution by the legislatures of the several States, as provided in the Constitution, within seven years from the date of the submission hereof to the States by the Congress.

AMENDMENT XIX

The right of citizens of the United States to vote shall not be denied or abridged by the United States or by any State on account of sex.

Congress shall have power to enforce this article by appropriate legislation.

AMENDMENT XX

Section 1: The terms of the President and Vice-President shall end at noon on the 20th day of January, and the terms of Senators and Representatives at noon on the 3rd day of January, of the years in which such terms would have ended if this article had not been ratified; and the terms of their successors shall then begin.

Section 2: The Congress shall assemble at least once in every year, and such meeting shall begin at noon on the 3rd day of January, unless they shall by law appoint a different day.

Section 3: If, at the time fixed for the beginning of the term of the President, the President elect shall have died, the Vice-President elect shall become President. If a President shall not have been chosen before the time fixed for the beginning of his term, or if the President elect shall have failed to qualify, then the Vice-President elect shall act as President until a President shall have qualified; and the Congress may by law provide for the case wherein neither a President elect nor a Vice-President elect shall have qualified, declaring who shall then act as President, or the manner in which one who is to act shall be selected, and such person shall act accordingly until a President or Vice-President shall have qualified.

Section 4: The Congress may by law provide for the case of the death of any of the persons from whom the

House of Representatives may choose a President whenever the right of choice shall have devolved upon them, and for the case of the death of any of the persons from whom the Senate may choose a Vice-President whenever the right of choice shall have devolved upon them.

Section 5: Sections 1 and 2 shall take effect on the 15th day of October following the ratification of this article.

Section 6: This article shall be inoperative unless it shall have been ratified as an amendment to the Constitution by the legislatures of three-fourths of the several States within seven years from the date of its submission.

AMENDMENT XXI

Section 1: The eighteenth article of amendment to the Constitution of the United States is hereby repealed.

Section 2: The transportation or importation into any State, Territory, or possession of the United States for delivery or use therein of intoxicating liquors, in violation of the laws thereof, is hereby prohibited.

Section 3: This article shall be inoperative unless it shall have been ratified as an amendment to the Constitution by conventions in the several States, as provided in the Constitution, within seven years from the date of the submission hereof to the States by the Congress.

AMENDMENT XXII

No person shall be elected to the office of the President more than twice, and no person who has held the office of President, or acted as President, for more than two years of a term to which some other person was elected President shall be elected to the office of the President more than once.

But this Article shall not apply to any person holding the office of President when this Article was proposed by the Congress, and shall not prevent any person who may be holding the office of President, or acting as President, during the term within which this Article becomes operative from holding the office of President or acting as President during the remainder of such term.

AMENDMENT XXIII

Section 1: The District constituting the seat of Government of the United States shall appoint in such manner as the Congress may direct:

A number of electors of President and Vice-President equal to the whole number of Senators and Representatives in Congress to which the District would be entitled if it were a State, but in no event more than the least populous State; they shall be in addition to those appointed by the States, but they shall be considered, for the purposes of the election of President and Vice President, to be electors appointed by a State; and they shall meet in the District and perform such duties as provided by the twelfth article of amendment.

Section 2: The Congress shall have power to enforce this article by appropriate legislation.

AMENDMENT XXIV

Section 1: The right of citizens of the United States to vote in any primary or other election for President or Vice-President, for electors for President or Vice-President, or for Senator or Representative in Congress, shall not be denied or abridged by the United States or any State by reason of failure to pay any poll tax or other tax.

Section 2: The Congress shall have the power to enforce this article by appropriate legislation.

AMENDMENT XXV

Section 1: In case of the removal of the President from office or his death or resignation, the Vice-President shall become President.

Section 2: Whenever there is a vacancy in the office of the Vice-President, the President shall nominate a Vice-President who shall take the office upon confirmation by a majority vote of both houses of Congress.

Section 3: Whenever the President transmits to the President pro tempore of the Senate and the Speaker of the House of Representatives his written declaration that he is unable to discharge the powers and duties of his office, and until he transmits to them a written declaration to the contrary, such powers and duties shall be discharged by the Vice-President as Acting President.

Section 4: Whenever the Vice-President and a majority of either the principal officers of the executive departments, or of such other body as Congress may by law provide, transmit to the President pro tempore of the Senate and the Speaker of the House of Representatives their written declaration that the President is unable to discharge the powers and duties of his office, the Vice-President shall immediately assume the powers and duties of the office as Acting President.

Thereafter, when the President transmits to the President pro tempore of the Senate and the Speaker of the House of Representatives his written declaration that no inability exists, he shall resume the powers and duties of his office unless the Vice-President and a majority of either the principal officers of the executive departments, or of such other body as Congress may by law provide, transmit within four days to the President pro tempore of the Senate and the Speaker of the House of Representatives their written declaration that the President is unable to discharge the powers and duties of his office. Thereupon Congress shall decide the issue, assembling within 48 hours for that purpose if not in session. If the Congress, within 21 days after receipt of the latter written declaration, or, if Congress is not in session, within 21 days after Congress is required to assemble, determines by two-thirds vote of both houses that the President is unable to discharge the powers and duties of his office, the Vice-President shall continue to discharge the same as Acting President; otherwise, the President shall resume the powers and duties of his office.

AMENDMENT XXVI

Section 1: The right of citizens of the United States, who are 18 years of age or older, to vote shall not be denied or abridged by the United States or any state on account of age.

Section 2: The Congress shall have the power to enforce this article by appropriate legislation.

AMENDMENT XXVII

No law varying the compensation for the services of the Senators and Representatives, shall take effect until an election of Representatives shall have intervened.

THE FORGOTTEN PRESIDENTS

Who was the first president of the United States? Ask any school-child and they will readily tell you "George Washington." And of course they would be wrong—at least technically. Washington was not inaugurated until April 30, 1789. And yet the United States continually had functioning governments from as early as September 5, 1774, and operated as a confederated nation from as early as July 4, 1776. During that nearly fifteen-year interval, Congress—first the Continental Congress and then the Confederation Congress—was always moderated by a duly elected president. As the chief executive officer of the government of the United States, the president was recognized as the head of state. Washington was thus the fifteenth in a long line of distinguished presidents; he just happened to be the first under the current Constitution. So who were the luminaries who preceded him? The following brief biographies profile these "forgotten presidents."

PEYTON RANDOLPH OF VIRGINIA (1723–75)

When delegates gathered in Philadelphia for the First Continental Congress, they promptly elected the former king's attorney of Virginia as the moderator and president of their convocation. He was a propitious choice—a legal prodigy who studied at the Inner Temple in London, served as his native colony's attorney general, and tutored many of the most able men of the South at William and Mary College, including the young Patrick Henry. His home in Williamsburg was the gathering place for Virginia's legal and political gentry, and it remains a popular attraction in the restored colonial capital. He had served as a delegate in the Virginia House of Burgesses, and had been a commander under William Byrd in the colonial militia. He was a scholar of some renown—having begun a self-guided reading of the classics when he was thirteen. Despite suffering poor health, he twice served as president in the Continental Congress, in 1774 from September 5 to October 21, and then again for a few days in 1775 from May 10 to May 23. He never lived to see independence, yet was numbered among the nation's most revered founders.

HENRY MIDDLETON (1717–84)

America's second elected president was one of the wealthiest planters in the South and the patriarch of one of the most powerful families anywhere in the nation. His public spirit was evident from an early age. He was a member of his state's Common House from 1744–47; during the last two years he served as the speaker. During 1755 he was the king's commissioner of Indian affairs. He was a member of the South Carolina Council from 1755 to 1770, and his valor in the war with the Cherokees during 1760–61 demonstrated his cool leadership abilities while under pressure and earned him wide recognition throughout the colonies. He was elected as a delegate to the first session of the Continental Congress, and when Peyton Randolph was forced to resign the presidency, his peers immediately turned to Middleton to complete the term. He served as the fledgling coalition's president from October 22, 1774, until Randolph was able to briefly resume his duties on May 10, 1775. Afterward he was a member of the Congressional Council of Safety and helped to establish the young nation's policy toward the encouragement and support of education. In February 1776 he resigned his political involvements in order to prepare his family and lands for what he believed was inevitable war. He was replaced by his son Arthur, who eventually became a signer of both the Declaration of Independence and the Articles of Confederation, served time as an English prisoner of war, and was twice elected governor of his state.

JOHN HANCOCK (1737–93)

The third president was a patriot, rebel leader, and merchant who with giant strokes signed his name into immortality on the Declaration of Independence. The boldness of his signature has lived in American minds as a perfect expression of the strength and freedom—and defiance—of the individual in the face of British tyranny. As president of the Continental Congress during two

widely spaced terms—the first from May 24, 1775, to
October 30, 1777, and the second from November 23,
1785, to June 5, 1786—Hancock was the presiding officer when members approved the Declaration of Independence. Because of his position, it was his official duty to
sign the document first (but not necessarily as dramatically as he did). Hancock figured prominently in another
historic event—the battle at Lexington. British troops
who fought there on April 10, 1775, had known Hancock
and Samuel Adams were in Lexington and had gone
there to capture these rebel leaders. The two would have
been captured if they had not been warned by Paul
Revere. As early as 1768 Hancock defied the British by
refusing to pay customs charges on the cargo of one of his
ships. One of Boston's wealthiest merchants, he was recognized by the citizens as well as the British as a rebel
leader and was elected president of the first Massachusetts provincial congress. After he was chosen president
of the Continental Congress in 1775, Hancock became
known beyond the borders of Massachusetts. Having
served as colonel of the Massachusetts Governor's
Guards, he hoped to be named commander of the American forces—until John Adams nominated George
Washington. In 1778 Hancock was commissioned major
general and took part in an unsuccessful campaign in
Rhode Island. But it was as a political leader that his real
distinction was earned, as the first governor of Massachusetts, as president of Congress, and as president of the

Massachusetts constitutional ratification convention. He helped win ratification in Massachusetts, gaining enough popular recognition to make him a contender for the newly created presidency of the United States, but again he saw Washington gain the prize. Like his rival, George Washington, Hancock was a wealthy man who risked much for the cause of independence. Indeed, he was the wealthiest New Englander supporting the patriotic cause, and although he lacked the brilliance of John Adams or Samuel Adams's capacity to inspire, he became one of the foremost leaders of the new nation, perhaps in part because he was willing to commit so much, and at such risk, to the cause of freedom.

HENRY LAURENS (1724–92)

The only American president ever to be held as a prisoner of war by a foreign power, after he was released Laurens was heralded as "the father of our country" by no less a personage than George Washington. He was of Huguenot extraction, his ancestors having come to America from France after the revocation of the Edict of Nantes made the Reformed faith illegal. Raised and educated for a life of mercantilism at his home in Charleston, he also had the opportunity to spend more than a year in continental travel. It was while in Europe that he began to write revolutionary pamphlets, gaining him renown as a patriot. He served as vice president of South Carolina in 1776. He was then elected to the Continental Congress. He succeeded

John Hancock as president of the newly independent but war-beleaguered United States on November 1, 1777, and served until December 9, 1778, at which time he was appointed ambassador to the Netherlands. Unfortunately for the cause of the young nation, he was captured by an English warship during his cross-Atlantic voyage and was confined to the Tower of London until the end of the war. After the battle of Yorktown, the American government regained his freedom in a dramatic prisoner exchange—Laurens for Lord Cornwallis. Ever the patriot, Laurens continued to serve his nation as one of the three representatives selected to negotiate terms at the Paris peace conference in 1782.

JOHN JAY (1745–1829)

America's first secretary of state, first chief justice of the Supreme Court, one of its first ambassadors, and author of some of the celebrated Federalist Papers, Jay was a Founding Father who, by a quirk of fate, missed signing the Declaration of Independence—at the time of the vote for independence and the signing, he had temporarily left the Continental Congress to serve in New York's revolutionary legislature. Nevertheless, he was chosen by his peers to succeed Henry Laurens as president of the United States—serving a term from December 10, 1778, to September 27, 1779. A conservative New York lawyer who was at first against the idea of independence for the colonies, the aristocratic Jay in 1776 became a patriot who was willing to give the next twenty-five years of his life to help establish the new nation. During those years he won the regard of his peers as a dedicated and accomplished statesman and a man of unwavering principle. In the Continental Congress Jay prepared addresses to the people of Canada and Great Britain. In New York he drafted the state constitution and served as chief justice during the war. He was president of the Continental Congress before he undertook the difficult assignment, as ambassador, of trying to gain support and funds from Spain. After helping Franklin, Jefferson, Adams, and Laurens complete peace negotiations in Paris in 1783, Jay returned to become the first secretary of state, then called the "Secretary of Foreign Affairs" under the Articles of Confederation. He negotiated valuable commercial treaties with Russia and Morocco and dealt with the continuing controversy with Britain and Spain over the southern and western boundaries of the United States; he proposed that America and Britain establish a joint commission to arbitrate disputes that remained after the war—a proposal that, though not adopted, influenced the government's use of arbitration and diplomacy in settling later international problems. In this post Jay felt keenly the weakness of the Articles of Confederation and was one of the first to advocate a new governmental compact. He wrote five Federalist Papers supporting the Constitution, and he was a leader in the New York Ratification Convention. As first chief justice of the Supreme Court,

Jay made the historic decision that a state could be sued by a citizen from another state, which led to the Eleventh Amendment to the Constitution. On a special mission to London he concluded the "Jay Treaty," helping avert a renewal of hostilities with Britain but winning little popular favor at home. It is probably for this treaty that this Founding Father is best remembered.

SAMUEL HUNTINGTON (1732–96)

An industrious youth who mastered his studies of the law without the advantage of a school, a tutor, or a master, borrowing books and snatching opportunities to read and research between odd jobs, he was one of the greatest self-made men among the Founders. He was also one of the greatest legal minds of the age—all the more remarkable for his lack of advantage as a youth. In 1764, in recognition of his obvious abilities and initiative, he was elected to the General Assembly of Connecticut. The next year he was chosen to serve on the Executive Council. In 1774 he was appointed associate judge of the Superior Court, and as a delegate to the Continental Congress he was acknowledged to be a legal scholar of some respect. He served in Congress for five consecutive terms, during the last of which he was elected president, serving in that office from September 28, 1779, until ill health forced him to resign on July 9, 1781. He returned to his home in Connecticut, and as he recuperated, he accepted more conciliar and bench duties. He again took his seat in Congress in 1783, but left it to become chief justice of his state's superior court. He was elected lieutenant governor in 1785 and governor in 1786. According to John Jay, he was "the most precisely trained Christian jurist ever to serve his country."

THOMAS MCKEAN (1734–1817)

During his astonishingly varied fifty-year career in public life he held almost every possible position, from deputy county attorney to president of the United States under the Confederation. Besides signing the Declaration of Independence, he contributed significantly to the development and establishment of constitutional government in both his home state of Delaware and the nation. At the Stamp Act Congress he proposed the voting procedure that Congress adopted: each colony, regardless of size or population, had one vote—the practice adopted by the Continental Congress and the Congress of the Confederation and the principle of state equality manifest in the composition of the Senate. And as county judge in 1765, he defied the British by ordering his court to work only with documents that did not bear the hated stamps. In June 1776, at the Continental Congress, McKean joined with Caesar Rodney to register Delaware's approval (over the negative vote of the third Delaware delegate, George Read) of the Declaration of Independence, permitting it to be "the unanimous declaration of the thirteen United States." At a special Delaware convention he drafted the constitution for that state. McKean also helped draft—and signed—the Articles of Confederation. It was during his tenure of service as president—from July 10, 1781, to November 4, 1782—that news arrived from General Washington in October 1781 that the British had surrendered following the battle of Yorktown. As chief justice of the supreme court of Pennsylvania, he contributed to the establishment of the legal system in that state, and in 1787 he strongly supported the Constitution at the Pennsylvania Ratification Convention, declaring it "the best the world has yet seen." At sixty-five, after more than forty years of public service, McKean resigned from his post as chief justice. A candidate on the Democratic-Republican ticket in 1799, McKean was elected governor of Pennsylvania and followed such a strict policy of appointing only fellow Republicans to office that he became the father of the spoils system in America. He served three tempestuous terms as governor, completing one of the longest continuous careers of public service of any of the Founding Fathers.

JOHN HANSON (1715–83)

He was the heir of one of the greatest family traditions in the colonies and became the patriarch of a long line of American patriots. His great-grandfather died at Lutzen beside the great King Gustavus Aldophus of Sweden; his grandfather was one of the founders of New Sweden along the Delaware River in Maryland.

One of his nephews was the military secretary to George Washington. Another was a signer of the Declaration; one was a signer of the Constitution; and one was governor of Maryland during the Revolution; and still another was a member of the First Congress. Two of his sons were killed in action with the Continental Army, a grandson served as a member of Congress under the new Constitution, and another grandson was a Maryland senator. Thus, even if Hanson had not served as president himself, he would have greatly contributed to the life of the nation through his ancestry and progeny. As a youngster he began a self-guided reading of classics and rather quickly became an acknowledged expert in the jurisprudence of Anselm and the practical philosophy of Seneca—both of whom influenced the political philosophy of the great leaders of the Reformation. It was based upon these legal and theological studies that the young planter (his farm, Mulberry Grove, was just across the Potomac from Mount Vernon) began to espouse the cause of the patriots. In 1775 he was elected to the provincial legislature of Maryland. In 1777 he became a member of Congress, where he distinguished himself as a brilliant administrator. He was elected president in 1781, where he served from November 5, 1781, until November 3, 1782. He was the first president to serve a full term after the full ratification of the Articles of Confederation, and like so many of the Southern and New England Founders, he was strongly opposed to the

Constitution when it was first discussed. He remained a confirmed anti-Federalist until his untimely death.

ELIAS BOUDINOT (1741–1802)

He did not sign the Declaration, the Articles, or the Constitution. He did not serve in the Continental Army with distinction. He was not renowned for his legal mind or his political skills. He was, instead, a man who spent his entire career in foreign diplomacy. He earned the respect of his fellow patriots during the dangerous days following the traitorous action of Benedict Arnold. His deft handling of relations with Canada also earned him great praise. After being elected to Congress from his home state of New Jersey, he served as the new nation's secretary for foreign affairs—managing the influx of aid from France, Spain, and Holland. In 1782 he was elected to the presidency and served in that office from November 4, 1782, until November 2, 1783. Like so many of the other early presidents, he was a classically trained scholar, a practitioner of the Reformed faith, and an anti-Federalist in political matters. He was the father and grandfather of frontiersmen; one of his grandchildren and namesakes eventually became a leader of the Cherokee nation in its bid for independence from the sprawling expansion of the United States.

THOMAS MIFFLIN (1744–1800)

By an ironic sort of providence, Thomas Mifflin served as George Washington's first aide-de-camp at the beginning of the Revolutionary War, and when the war was over, he was the man, as president of the United States, who accepted Washington's resignation of his commission. In the years between Mifflin greatly served the cause of freedom—and apparently his own cause—while serving as the first quartermaster general of the Continental Army. He obtained desperately needed supplies for the new army and was suspected of making excessive profit himself. Although experienced in business and successful in obtaining supplies for the war, Mifflin preferred the front lines, and he distinguished himself in military actions on Long Island and near Philadelphia. Born and reared a Quaker, he was excluded from their meetings for his military activities. He was a controversial figure who lost favor with Washington and was part of the Conway Cabal, a rather notorious plan to replace Washington with General Horatio Gates. Mifflin narrowly missed court-martialing over his handling of funds by resigning his commission in 1778. In spite of these problems (and repeated charges that he was a drunkard) Mifflin continued to be elected to positions of responsibility—as president and governor of Pennsylvania and delegate to the Constitutional Convention, and in the highest office in the land, where he served from November 3, 1783, to November 29, 1784. Most of Mifflin's significant contributions occurred in his earlier years; in the First and Second Continental Congresses he was firm in his stand for independence and for fighting for it, and he helped obtain both men and supplies for Washington's army in the early critical period. In 1784, as president, he signed the treaty with Great Britain that ended the war. Although a delegate to the Constitutional Convention, he did not make a significant contribution beyond signing the document. As governor of Pennsylvania, although he was accused of negligence, he supported improvements of roads and reformed the state penal and judicial systems. Despite the fact that he had gradually become sympathetic to Jefferson's principles regarding state's rights, he directed the Pennsylvania militia to support the federal tax collectors in the Whiskey Rebellion. In spite of charges of corruption, the affable Mifflin remained a popular figure. His magnetic personality and effective speaking ability led him to hold a variety of elective offices for almost thirty years of the critical Revolutionary period.

RICHARD HENRY LEE (1732–94)

Approved by the Continental Congress on July 2, 1776, Lee's resolution "that these United Colonies are, and of right ought to be, free and independent States," was the first official act of the United Colonies that set them irrevocably on the road to independence. It was not surprising that it came from Lee's pen; as early as 1768 he proposed the idea of committees of correspondence among the colonies, and in 1774 he proposed that the colonies meet in what became the Continental Congress.

From the first his eye was on independence. A wealthy Virginia planter whose ancestors had been granted extensive lands by King Charles II, Lee disdained the traditional aristocratic role and view. In the House of Burgesses he flatly denounced the practice of slavery. He saw independent America as "an asylum where the unhappy may find solace, and the persecuted repose." In 1764, when news of the proposed Stamp Act reached Virginia, Lee was a member of the committee of the House of Burgesses that drew up an address to the king—an official protest against such a tax. After the tax was established, Lee organized the citizens of his county into the Westmoreland Association, a group pledged to buy no British goods until the Stamp Act was repealed. At the First Continental Congress, Lee persuaded representatives from all the colonies to adopt his nonimportation idea, leading to the formation of the Continental Association, which was one of the first steps toward union of the colonies. Lee also proposed to the First Continental Congress that a militia be organized and armed—the year before the first shots were fired at Lexington—but this and other proposals of his were considered too radical at the time. Three days after Lee introduced his resolution in June of 1776, he was appointed by Congress to the committee responsible for drafting a declaration of independence, but he was called home when his wife fell ill, and his place was taken by his young protégé, Thomas Jefferson. Thus Lee missed the chance to draft the document, though his influence greatly shaped it and he was able to return in time to sign it. He was elected president, serving from November 30, 1784, to November 22, 1785, when he was succeeded by the second administration of John Hancock. Elected to the Constitutional Convention, Lee refused to attend, but as a member of the Congress of the Confederation, he contributed to another great document, the Northwest Ordinance, which provided for the formation of new states from the Northwest Territory. When the completed Constitution was sent to the states for ratification, Lee opposed it as antidemocratic and anti-Christian. However, as one of Virginia's first senators, he helped assure passage of the Bill of Rights amendments that he felt corrected many of the document's gravest faults. He was the great-uncle of Robert E. Lee and the scion of a great family tradition.

NATHANIEL GORHAM (1738–96)

Another self-made man, Gorham was one of the many successful Boston merchants who risked all he had for the cause of freedom. He was first elected to the Massachusetts general court in 1771, where his honesty and integrity won him acclaim. He was thus among the first delegates chosen to serve in the Continental Congress. He remained in public service throughout the war and into the Constitutional period, though his greatest contribution was his call for a stronger central government.

But even though he was an avid Federalist, he did not believe that the union could—or even should—be maintained peaceably for more than a hundred years. He was convinced that eventually, in order to avoid civil or cultural war, smaller regional interests should pursue an independent course. His support of a new constitution was rooted more in pragmatism than ideology. When John Hancock was unable to complete his second term as president, Gorham was elected to succeed him, serving from June 6, 1786, to February 1, 1787. It was during this time that the Congress actually entertained the idea of asking Prince Henry (the brother of Frederick II of Prussia) and Bonnie Prince Charlie (the leader of the ill-fated Scottish Jacobite Rising and heir of the Stuart royal line) to consider the possibility of establishing a constitutional monarchy in America. It was a plan that had much to recommend it, but eventually the advocates of republicanism held the day. During the final years of his life, Gorham was concerned with several speculative land deals that nearly cost him his entire fortune.

ARTHUR ST. CLAIR (1734–1818)

Born and educated in Edinburgh, Scotland, during the tumultuous days of the final Jacobite Rising and the Tartan Suppression, St. Clair was the only president of the United States born and bred on foreign soil. Though most of his family and friends abandoned their devastated homeland in the years following the battle of Culloden—after which nearly a third of the land was depopulated through emigration to America—he stayed behind to learn the ways of the hated Hanoverian English in the Royal Navy. His plan was to study the enemy's military might in order to fight another day. During the global conflict of the Seven Years' War, generally known as the French and Indian War, he was stationed in the American theater. Afterward he decided to settle in Pennsylvania, where many of his kin had established themselves. His civic-mindedness quickly became apparent: he helped to organize both the New Jersey and the Pennsylvania militias, led the Continental Army's Canadian expedition, and was elected to Congress; his long years of training in the enemy camp were finally paying off. He was elected president in 1787, and he served from February 2 of that year until January 21 of the next. Following his term of duty in the highest office in the land, he became the first governor of the Northwest Territory and the founder of Cincinnati. Though he briefly supported the idea of creating a constitutional monarchy under the Stuarts' Bonnie Prince Charlie, he was a strident anti-Federalist, believing that the proposed federal constitution would eventually allow for the intrusion of government into virtually every sphere and aspect of life. He even predicted that under the vastly expanded centralized power of the state, the taxing powers of bureaucrats and other unelected officials would eventually confiscate as much as a quarter of the income of the citizens—a notion that seemed laughable at the time but that has proved to be ominously modest in light of our current governmental leviathan. St. Clair lived to see the hated English tyrants who destroyed his homeland defeated. But he despaired that his adopted home might actually create and impose similar tyrannies upon themselves.

WASHINGTON'S FAREWELL ADDRESS

By September 17, 1796, when this address was delivered to George Washington's cabinet in Philadelphia, the president had already served two terms and did not wish to serve a third. His immense popularity had dwindled dramatically due to his fierce federalism and his opposition to the formation of political parties that were emerging. In addition, he was tired of being lampooned in the political press. He considered this message so important that he had the full text published in newspapers around the country two days later so it would reach a much wider audience. The address warned against foreign involvements, political factions, and sectionalism and promoted religion, morality, and education.

Friends and fellow citizens: The period for a new election of a citizen to administer the executive government of the United States being not far distant, and the time actually arrived when your thoughts must be employed in designating the person who is to be clothed with that important trust, it appears to me proper, especially as it may conduce to a more distinct expression of the public voice, that I should now apprise you of the resolution I have formed to decline being considered among the number of those out of whom a choice is to be made.

In looking forward to the moment which is intended to terminate the career of my political life, my feelings do not permit me to suspend the deep acknowledgment of that debt of gratitude which I owe to my beloved country for the many honors it has conferred upon me; still more for the steadfast confidence with which it has supported me, and for the opportunities I have thence enjoyed of manifesting my inviolable attachment by services faithful and persevering, though in usefulness unequal to my zeal.

Here, perhaps, I ought to stop. But a solicitude for your welfare, which cannot end but with my life, and the apprehension of danger natural to that solicitude urge me on an occasion like the present to offer to your solemn contemplation and to recommend to your frequent review some sentiments which are the result of much reflection, of no inconsiderable observation, and which appear to me all important to the permanency of your felicity as a people.

The unity of government which constitutes you one people is also now dear to you. It is justly so, for it is a main pillar in the edifice of your real independence, the support of your tranquillity at home, your peace abroad, of your safety, of your prosperity, of that very liberty which you so highly prize.

But as it is easy to foresee that from different causes and from different quarters much pains will be taken, many artifices employed, to weaken in your minds the conviction of this truth, as this is the point in your political fortress against which the batteries of internal and external enemies will be most constantly and actively (though often covertly and insidiously) directed, it is of infinite moment that you should properly estimate the immense value of your national union to your collective and individual happiness.

The name of American, which belongs to you in your national capacity, must always exalt the just pride of patriotism more than any appellation derived from local discriminations. With slight shades of difference, you have the same religion, manners, habits, and political principles. You have in a common cause fought and triumphed together. The independence and liberty you possess are the work of joint councils and joint efforts, of common dangers, sufferings, and successes.

But these considerations, however powerfully they address themselves to your sensibility, are greatly outweighed by those which apply more immediately to your interest. Here every portion of our country finds the most commanding motives for carefully guarding and preserving the union of the whole.

In contemplating the causes which may disturb our Union, it occurs as matter of serious concern that any ground should have been furnished for characterizing parties by geographical discriminations—Northern and Southern, Atlantic and Western—whence designing men may endeavor to excite a belief that there is a real difference of local interests and views. One of the expedients of party to acquire influence within particular districts is to misrepresent the opinions and aims of other districts. You cannot shield yourselves too much against the jealousies and heartburnings which spring from these misrepresentations. They tend to render alien to each other those who ought to be bound together by fraternal affection.

To the efficacy and permanency of your Union a government for the whole is indispensable. No alliances, however strict, between the parts can be an adequate substitute. They must inevitably experience the infractions and interruptions which all alliances in all times have experienced. Sensible of this momentous truth, you have improved upon your first essay by the adoption of a constitution of government better calculated than your former for an intimate union, and for the efficacious management of your common concerns.

Toward the preservation of your government and the permanency of your present happy state, it is requisite not only that you steadily discountenance irregular oppositions to its acknowledged authority, but also that you resist with care the spirit of innovation upon its principles, however specious the pretexts. One method of assault may be to effect in the forms of the Constitution alterations which will impair the energy of the system, and thus to undermine what cannot be directly overthrown.

I have already intimated to you the danger of parties in the state, with particular reference to the founding of them on geographical discriminations. Let me now take a more comprehensive view and warn you in the most solemn manner against the baneful effects of the spirit of party generally.

The alternate domination of one faction over another, sharpened by the spirit of revenge natural to party dissension, which in different ages and countries has perpetrated the most horrid enormities, is itself a frightful despotism. But this leads at length to a more formal and permanent despotism. The disorders and miseries which result gradually incline the minds of men to seek security and repose in the absolute power of an individual, and sooner or later the chief of some prevailing faction, more able or more fortunate than his competitors, turns this disposition to the purposes of his own elevation on the ruins of public liberty.

Of all the dispositions and habits which lead to political prosperity, religion and morality are indispensable supports. In vain would that man claim the tribute of patriotism who should labor to subvert these great pillars of human happiness, these firmest props of the duties of men and citizens. The mere politician, equally with the pious man, ought to respect and to cherish them. A volume could not trace all their connections with private and public felicity. Let it simply be asked: Where is the security for property, for reputation, for life, if the sense of religious obligation desert the oaths which are the instruments of investigation in courts of justice? And let us with caution indulge the supposition that morality can be maintained without religion. Whatever may be conceded to the influence of refined education on minds of peculiar structure, reason and experience both forbid us to expect that national morality can prevail in exclusion of religious principle.

'Tis substantially true that virtue or morality is a necessary spring of popular government. The rule indeed extends with more or less force to every species of free government. Who that is a sincere friend to it can look with indifference upon attempts to shake the foundation of the fabric? Promote, then, as an object of primary importance, institutions for the general diffusion of knowledge. In proportion as the structure of a government gives force to public opinion, it is essential that public opinion should be enlightened.

Observe good faith and justice toward all nations. Cultivate peace and harmony with all. Religion and morality enjoin this conduct; and can it be that good policy does not equally enjoin it? It will be worthy of a free, enlightened, and at no distant period, a great nation, to give to mankind the magnanimous and too novel example of a people always guided by an exalted justice and benevolence. Who can doubt that in the course of time and things the fruits of such a plan would richly repay any temporary advantages which might be lost by a steady adherence to it? Can it be that Providence has not connected the permanent felicity of a nation with its virtues? The experiment, at least, is recommended by every sentiment which ennobles human nature. Alas! is it rendered impossible by its vices?

In the execution of such a plan nothing is more essential than that permanent, inveterate antipathies against particular nations and passionate attachments for others should be excluded, and that in place of them just and amicable feelings toward all should be cultivated.

Harmony, liberal intercourse with all nations are recommended by policy, humanity, and interest. But even our commercial policy should hold an equal and impartial hand, neither seeking nor granting exclusive favors or preferences. There can be no greater error than to expect or calculate upon real favors from nation to nation. 'Tis an illusion which experience must cure, which a just pride ought to discard.

In offering to you, my countrymen, these counsels of an old and affectionate friend, I dare not hope they will make the strong and lasting impression I could wish, that they will control the usual current of the passions or prevent our nation from running the course which has hitherto marked the destiny of nations. But if I may even flatter myself that they may be productive of some partial benefit, some occasional good—that they may now and then recur to moderate the fury of party spirit, to warn against the mischiefs of foreign intrigue, to guard against the impostures of pretended patriotism—this hope will be a full recompense for the solicitude for your welfare by which they have been dictated.

Though in reviewing the incidents of my administration I am unconscious of intentional error, I am nevertheless too sensible of my defects not to think it probable that I may have committed many errors. Whatever they may be, I fervently beseech the Almighty to avert or mitigate the evils to which they may tend. I shall also carry with me the hope that my country will never cease to view them with indulgence, and that after forty-five years of my life dedicated to its service, with an upright zeal, the faults of incompetent abilities will be consigned to oblivion, as myself must soon be to the mansions of rest.

Relying on its kindness in this as in other things, and actuated by that fervent love toward it which is so natural to a man who views in it the native soil of himself and his progenitors for several generations, I anticipate with pleasing expectation that retreat in which I promise myself to realize, without alloy, the sweet enjoyment of partaking, in the midst of my fellow citizens, the benign influence of good laws under a free government—the ever favorite object of my heart and the happy reward, as I trust, of our mutual cares, labors, and dangers.

MY COUNTRY 'TIS OF THEE

Actually written prior to the Civil War, this hymnlike patriotic song by Samuel Smith became an anthem of healing in the years immediately following the terrible conflict. It very nearly became the national anthem during the Spanish–American War at the end of the nineteenth century due to its universal popularity. It seemed to express both an appreciation of the past and an optimism for the future.

My country 'tis of thee
Sweet land of liberty:
Of thee I sing.
Land where my fathers died
Land of the Pilgrims' pride
From every mountainside
Let freedom ring.

My native country thee
Land of the noble free
Thy name I love;
I love thy rocks and rills
Thy woods and templed hills
My heart with rapture thrills
Like that above.

Let music swell the breeze
And ring from all the trees
Sweet freedom's song
Let all that breathe partake
Let mortal tongues awake
Let rocks their silence break
The sound prolong.

Our fathers' God to thee
Author of liberty
To thee we sing
Long may our land be bright
With freedom's holy light
Protect us by thy might
Great God, our King.

THE STAR-SPANGLED BANNER

During the night of September 13, 1814, Francis Scott Key, a Washington attorney, was sent to the British command to secure the release of a prisoner when the fleet began to bombard the placements of American fortifications in Baltimore at Fort McHenry. Although the battle raged through the night, the defenses stood firm. The sight of the flag still flying over the fort the next morning inspired the young lawyer to pen these words. Set to a popular English song, "Anacreon in Heaven," it was officially declared to be the national anthem more than a hundred years later, just before the First World War.

O! say, can you see, by the dawn's early light,
What so proudly we hailed at the twilight's last gleaming:
Whose broad stripes and bright stars, through the perilous
     fight,
O'er the ramparts we watched were so gallantly streaming,
And the rocket's red glare, the bombs bursting in air,
Gave proof through the night that our flag was still there:

O! say, does the star-spangled banner still wave
O'er the land of the free and the home of the brave?

On the shore, dimly seen through the mist of the deep,
Where the foe's haughty host in dread silence reposes,

What is that which the breeze, o'er the towering steep,
As it fitfully blows, half conceals, half discloses?
Now it catches the gleam of the morning's first beam—
In full glory reflected, now shines on the stream.

'Tis the star-spangled banner, O! long may it wave
O'er the land of the free and the home of the brave.

And where is the band who so vauntingly swore
That the havoc of war and the battle's confusion
A home and a country would leave us no more?
Their blood has washed out their foul footsteps' pollution.
No refuge could save the hireling and slave
From the terror of flight or the gloom of the grave!

And the star-spangled banner in triumph cloth wave
O'er the land of the free and the home of the brave.

O! thus be it ever when freemen shall stand
Between their loved homes and the foe's desolation;
Bless'd with victory and peace, may our heaven-rescued land
Praise the Power that hath made and preserved us a nation.
Then conquer we must, for our cause it is just—
And this be our motto—"In God is our trust!"

And the star-spangled banner in triumph shall wave
O'er the land of the free and the home of the brave.

A HOUSE DIVIDED

At the Illinois state Republican convention on June 7, 1858, a somewhat obscure Springfield attorney and failed politician made a startling speech that ultimately electrified the nation. Decrying the halfhearted attempts at compromise over the slavery issue—and particularly the infamous Dred Scott case— Abraham Lincoln made an incendiary case for enforced unity on the issue. It was this speech more than anything else that ultimately provoked the secession of the Southern states two years later.

Mr. President and Gentlemen of the Convention: If we could first know where we are, and whither we are tending, we could better judge what to do, and how to do it. We are now far into the fifth year since a policy was initiated with the avowed object and confident promise of putting an end to slavery agitation. Under the operation of that policy, that agitation has not only not ceased but has constantly augmented. In my opinion, it will not ease until a crisis shall have been reached and passed.

"A house divided against itself cannot stand." I believe this government cannot endure permanently half slave and half free. I do not expect the Union to be dissolved; I do not expect the house to fall; but I do expect it will cease to be divided. It will become all one thing, or all the other. Either the opponents of slavery will arrest the further spread of it, and place it where the public mind shall rest in the belief that it is in the course of ultimate extinction, or its advocates will push it forward till it shall become alike lawful in all the states, old as well as new, North as well as South.

Have we no tendency to the latter condition?

Let anyone who doubts carefully contemplate that now almost complete legal combination—piece of machinery, so to speak—compounded of the Nebraska doctrine and the Dred Scott decision. Let him consider not only what work the machinery is adapted to do, and how well adapted, but also let him study the history of its construction, and trace, if he can, or rather fail, if he can, to trace the evidences of design, and concert of action, among its chief architects, from the beginning.

The new year of 1854 found slavery excluded from more than half the states by state constitutions, and from most of the national territory by congressional prohibition. Four days later commenced the struggle which ended in repealing that congressional prohibition. This opened all the national territory to slavery and was the first point gained. . . .

While the Nebraska Bill was passing through Congress, a law case, involving the question of a Negro's freedom, by reason of his owner having voluntarily taken him first into a free state, and then into a territory covered by the congressional prohibition, and held him as a slave for a long time in each, was passing through the United States Circuit Court for the District of Missouri; and both Nebraska Bill and lawsuit were brought to a decision in the same month of May 1854. The Negro's name was Dred Scott, which name now designates the decision finally made in the case. Before the then next presidential election, the law case came to, and was argued in, the Supreme Court of the United States; but the decision of it was deferred until after the election.

The election came. Mr. Buchanan was elected, and the endorsement, such as it was, secured. That was the second point gained.

The reputed author of the Nebraska Bill finds an early occasion to make a speech at this capital endorsing the Dred Scott decision, and vehemently denouncing all opposition to it. The new president, too, seizes the early occasion of the Silliman letter to endorse and strongly construe that decision, and to express his astonishment that any different view had ever been entertained!

The several points of the Dred Scott decision, in connection with Senator Douglas's "care not" policy, constitute the piece of machinery, in its present state of advancement. This was the third point gained. The working points of that machinery are:

Firstly, That no Negro slave, imported as such from Africa, and no descendant of such slave, can ever be a citizen of any state, in the sense of that term as used in the

Constitution of the United States. This point is made in order to deprive the Negro, in every possible event, of the benefit of that provision of the United States Constitution which declares that "the citizens of each state shall be entitled to all privileges and immunities of citizens in the several states."

Secondly, That, "subject to the Constitution of the United States," neither Congress nor a territorial legislature can exclude slavery from any United States territory. This point is made in order that individual men may fill up the territories with slaves, without danger of losing them as property, and thus to enhance the chances of permanency to the institution through all the future.

Thirdly, That whether the holding a Negro in actual slavery in a free state makes him free, as against the holder, the United States courts will not decide, but will leave to be decided by the courts of any slave state the Negro may be forced into by the master. This point is made, not to be pressed immediately; but, if acquiesced in for a while, and apparently endorsed by the people at an election, then to sustain the logical conclusion that what Dred Scott's master might lawfully do with Dred Scott in the free state of Illinois, every other master may lawfully do with any other one, or one thousand slaves, in Illinois, or in any other free state.

It will throw additional light on the latter, to go back and run the mind over the string of historical facts already stated. Several things will now appear less dark and mysterious than they did when they were transpiring. The people were to be left "perfectly free," "subject only to the Constitution." What the Constitution had to do with it outsiders could not then see. Plainly enough now, it was an exactly fitted niche for the Dred Scott decision afterward to come in and declare that perfect freedom of the people to be just no freedom at all. Why was the amendment expressly declaring the right of the people to exclude slavery voted down? Plainly enough now, the adoption of it would have spoiled the niche for the Dred Scott decision. Why was the court decision held up? Why even a senator's individual opinion withheld till after the presidential election? Plainly enough now, the speaking out then would have damaged the "perfectly free" argument upon which the election was to be carried. Why the outgoing president's felicitation on the endorsement? Why the delay of a re-argument? Why the incoming president's advance exhortation in favor of the decision?

We cannot absolutely know that all these exact adaptations are the result of preconcert. But when we see a lot of framed timbers, different portions of which we know have been gotten out at different times and places and by different workmen—Stephen, Franklin, Roger, and James, for instance—and when we see these timbers joined together, and see they exactly make the frame of a house or a mill, all the tenons and mortices exactly fitting, and all the lengths and proportions of the different pieces exactly adapted to their respective places, and not a piece too many or too few, not omitting even scaffolding—or, if a single piece be lacking, we see the place in the frame exactly fitted and prepared to yet bring such piece in—in such a case we find it impossible not to believe that Stephen and Franklin and Roger and James all understood one another from the beginning, and all worked upon a common plan or draft drawn up before the first blow was struck.

While the opinion of the court, by Chief Justice Taney, in the Dred Scott case, and the separate opinions of all the concurring judges, expressly declare that the Constitution of the United States neither permits Congress nor a territorial legislature to exclude slavery from any United States territory, they all omit to declare whether or not the same Constitution permits a state, or the people of a state, to exclude it. We may, ere long, see another Supreme Court decision declaring that the Constitution of the United States does not permit a state to exclude slavery from its limits. And this may especially be expected if the doctrine of "care not whether slavery be voted down or voted up" shall gain upon the public mind sufficiently to give promise that such a decision can be maintained when made.

Such a decision is all that slavery now lacks of being alike lawful in all the states. Welcome, or unwelcome, such decision is probably coming, and will soon be upon us, unless the power of the present political dynasty shall be met and overthrown. We shall lie down pleasantly dreaming that the people of Missouri are on the verge of making their state free, and we shall awake to the reality instead that the Supreme Court has made Illinois a slave state. To meet and overthrow the power of that dynasty is the work now before all those who would prevent that consummation. That is what we have to do. How can we best do it?

There are those who denounce us openly to their own friends, and yet whisper us softly that Senator Douglas is the aptest instrument there is with which to effect that object. They do not tell us, nor has he told us, that he wishes any such object to be effected. They wish us to infer all from the facts that he now has a little quarrel with the present head of the dynasty; and that he has regularly voted with us on a single point upon which he and we have never differed. They remind us that he is a very great man, and that the largest of us are very small ones. Let this be granted. But "a living dog is better than a dead lion." Judge Douglas, if not a dead lion for this work, is at least a caged and toothless one.

Our cause, then, must be entrusted to, and conducted by, its own undoubted friends—those whose hands are free, whose hearts are in the work, who do care for the result. Two years ago the Republicans of the nation mustered over thirteen hundred thousand strong. We did this under the single impulse of resistance to a common danger, with every external circumstance against us. Of strange, discordant, and even hostile elements, we gathered from the four winds, and formed and fought the battle through, under the constant hot fire of a disciplined, proud, and pampered enemy. Did we brave all then to falter now?

Now, when that same enemy is wavering, dissevered, and belligerent? The result is not doubtful. We shall not fail—if we stand firm, we shall not fail. Wise counsels may accelerate or mistakes delay it, but, sooner or later, the victory is sure to come.

THE SULLIVAN BALLOU LETTER

*In the trenches of the battlefield, soldiers' thoughts inevitably
turn toward home. Reading the correspondence of those who
wore blue or gray during the awful conflict of the Civil War is
a heart-rending experience. A glimpse of the pathos of that
tragic struggle was captured by Sullivan Ballou in this letter
written to his wife in 1861. A week later, the young major in
the Second Rhode Island Volunteers was killed at the battle of
Bull Run.*

The indications are very strong that we shall move in a few
days perhaps tomorrow.

Lest I shall not be able to write to you again, I feel
impelled to write a few lines that may fall under your eye
when I shall be no more.

Our movement may be one of a few days duration and
full of pleasure and it may be one of severe conflict and
death to me. "Not my will, but Thine O God be done." If
it is necessary that I should fall on the battlefield for my
Country, I am ready. I have no misgivings about or lack of

confidence in the cause in which I am engaged and my courage does not halt or falter.

I know how strongly American Civilization now leans upon the triumph of the Government, and how great a debt we owe to those who went before us through the blood and suffering of the Revolution, and I am willing, perfectly willing to lay down all my joys in this life to help maintain this Government and to pay that debt, but my dear wife when I know that with my own joys I lay down nearly all of yours and replace them in this life with cares and sorrows, when after having eaten for long years the bitter fruit of orphanage myself I must offer it as the only sustenance to my dear little children, is it weak or dishonorable that while the banner of my purpose floats calmly and proudly in the breeze underneath my unbounded love for you my darling wife and children, I shall struggle in fierce though useless contest with my love of Country.

I cannot describe to you my feelings on this calm summer Sabbath night when two thousand men are sleeping around me many of them enjoying the last perhaps before that of death; and I am suspicious that death is creeping behind me with his fatal dart while I am communing with God, My Country and Thee. I have sought most closely and diligently and often in my breast for a wrong motive in thus hazarding the happiness of all those I loved and I could not find one. A pure love of my Country and the principles I have often advocated before the people another name of honor that I love more than I fear death has called upon me and I have obeyed.

Sarah, my love for you is deathless, it seems to bind me in mighty cables that nothing but Omnipotence could break and my love of country comes over me like a strong wind and bears me irresistibly on with all these chains to the battlefield.

The memories of the blissful moments I have spent with you come creeping over me and I feel most deeply grateful to God and you that I have enjoyed them so long and how hard it is for me to give them up and burn to ashes the hopes of future years when God Willing we might still have lived and loved together and seen our boys grow up to honorable manhood around us.

I know I have but few and small claims upon Divine Providence but something whispers to me perhaps it is the wafted prayer of my little Edgar that I shall return to my loved ones unharmed. If I do not my dear Sarah never forget how much I love you and when my last breath escapes me on the battlefield I shall whisper your name. Forgive my many faults and the many pains I have caused you how thoughtless how foolish I have often times been. How gladly would I wash out with my tears every little spot upon your happiness and struggle with all the misfortunes of this world to shield you and my dear children from harm but I cannot I must watch you from the spirit land and hover near you while you buffet the storms with your precious little freight and wait with sad patience till we meet to part no more. But Oh Sarah if the dead can come back to this earth and flit unseen around those they love, I shall always be near you in the gladdest day and in the darkest night amidst your happiest scenes and gloomiest hours always, always and if there be a soft breeze upon your cheeks it shall be my breath or the cool air cools your throbbing temple, it shall be my spirit passing by.

Sarah, do not mourn me dead, think I am gone and wait for me, for we shall meet again.

As for my little boys, they will grow up as I have grown and never know a father's love and care, little Willie is too young to remember me long but my blue-eyed Edgar will keep my frolics with him among the dimmest memories of his childhood.

Sarah, I have unbounded confidence in your maternal care and your development of their characters and feel that God will bless you in your holy work.

Tell my two mothers I call God's blessings upon them.

Oh Sarah I wait for you there come to me and lead thither my children.

THE GETTYSBURG ADDRESS

Although he was not the main speaker at the dedication of a national cemetery on the site of the bloody Gettysburg battlefield, the tantalizingly short speech Abraham Lincoln gave on November 19, 1863, is a masterpiece of both penetrating rhetoric and moral politics. These words, although few, have proved to be immortal. Carl Sandburg in 1946 hailed the address as one of the great American poems. "One may delve deeply into its unfolded meanings," he wrote, "but its poetic significance carries it far beyond the limits of a state paper. It curiously incarnates the claims, assurances, and pretenses of republican institutions, of democratic procedure, of the rule of the people. It is a timeless psalm in the name of those who fight and do in behalf of great human causes rather than talk, in a belief that men can 'highly resolve' themselves, and can mutually 'dedicate' their lives to a cause."

Fourscore and seven years ago our fathers brought forth, on this continent, a new nation, conceived in liberty, and dedicated to the proposition that all men are created equal.

Now we are engaged in a great civil war, testing whether that nation, or any nation so conceived, and so dedicated, can long endure. We are met on a great battlefield of that war. We have come to dedicate a portion of that field, as a final resting place for those who here gave their lives, that that nation might live. It is altogether fitting and proper that we should do this.

But, in a larger sense, we can not dedicate—we can not consecrate—we can not hallow—this ground. The brave men, living and dead, who struggled here, have consecrated it far above our poor power to add or detract. The world will little note, nor long remember what we say here, but it can never forget what they did here. It is for us the living, rather, to be dedicated here to the unfinished work which they who fought here have thus far so nobly advanced. It is rather for us to be here dedicated to the great task remaining before us—that from these honored dead we take increased devotion to that cause for which they here gave the last full measure of devotion—that we here highly resolve that these dead shall not have died in vain—that this nation, under God, shall have a new birth of freedom—and that government of the people, by the people, for the people, shall not perish from the earth.

THE PLEDGE OF ALLEGIANCE

This patriotic vow was written by journalist Francis Bellamy to commemorate the four hundredth anniversary of the discovery voyage of Christopher Columbus in 1892. Although it was first publicly recited at the Columbian Exposition in Chicago that year, it was not officially recognized until 1954. At that time the original was revised to include the words "under God." Usually recited at the opening of public ceremonies or events, it is a kind of national covenantal commitment.

I pledge allegiance
To the flag of the United States of America
And to the republic for which it stands,
One nation under God,
Indivisible, with liberty, and justice for all.

ATLANTA EXPOSITION ADDRESS

*Born into slavery, Booker T. Washington literally pulled him-
self up by his own bootstraps to become one of the most articulate and influential educators in the nation. Founder of the
Tuskegee Institute, author of a number of books, and a popular
speaker, he always emphasized the importance of education,
hard work, and self-discipline for the advancement of African
Americans. Washington's audience at the Cotton States' Exposition on September 18, 1895, included both white and black
Southerners, and his speech received enormous attention
throughout the country; it helped galvanize public opinion in
favor of black self-improvement.*

Mr. President and Gentlemen of the Board of Directors
and Citizens: One-third of the population of the South is
of the Negro race. No enterprise seeking the material,
civil, or moral welfare of this section can disregard this
element of our population and reach the highest success. I
but convey to you, Mr. President and directors, the sentiment of the masses of my race when I say that in no way
have the value and manhood of the American Negro been
more fittingly and generously recognized than by the
managers of this magnificent exposition at every stage of
its progress. It is a recognition that will do more to cement

the friendship of the two races than any occurrence since the dawn of our freedom.

Not only this, but the opportunity here afforded will awaken among us a new era of industrial progress. Ignorant and inexperienced, it is not strange that in the first years of our new life we began at the top instead of at the bottom; that a seat in Congress or the state legislature was more sought than real estate or industrial skill; that the political convention or stump speaking had more attractions than starting a dairy farm or truck garden.

A ship lost at sea for many days suddenly sighted a friendly vessel. From the mast of the unfortunate vessel was seen a signal, "Water, water; we die of thirst!" The answer from the friendly vessel at once came back, "Cast down your bucket where you are." And a third and fourth signal for water was answered, "Cast down your bucket where you are." The captain of the distressed vessel, at last heeding the injunction, cast down his bucket, and it came up full of fresh, sparkling water from the mouth of the Amazon River. To those of my race who depend on bettering their condition in a foreign land or who underestimate the importance of cultivating friendly relations with the Southern white man, who is their next-door neighbor, I would say: "Cast down your bucket where you are"—cast it down in making friends in every manly way of the people of all races by whom we are surrounded.

Cast it down in agriculture, mechanics, in commerce, in domestic service, and in the professions. And in this connection it is well to bear in mind that whatever other sins the South may be called to bear, when it comes to business, pure and simple, it is in the South that the Negro is given a man's chance in the commercial world, and in nothing is this exposition more eloquent than in emphasizing this chance. Our greatest danger is that in the great leap from slavery to freedom we may overlook the fact that the masses of us are to live by the productions of our hands, and fail to keep in mind that we shall prosper in proportion as we learn to dignify and glorify common labor and put brains and skill into the common occupations of life; shall prosper in proportion as we learn to draw the line between the superficial and the substantial, the ornamental gew-gaws of life and the useful. No race can prosper till it learns that there is as much dignity in tilling a field as in writing a poem. It is at the bottom of life we must begin, and not at the top. Nor should we permit our grievances to overshadow our opportunities.

To those of the white race who look to the incoming of those of foreign birth and strange tongue and habits for the prosperity of the South, were I permitted I would repeat what I say to my own race, "Cast down your bucket where you are." Cast it down among the eight millions of Negroes whose habits you know, whose fidelity and love you have tested in days when to have proved treacherous meant the ruin of your firesides. Cast down your bucket among these people who have, without strikes and labor wars, tilled your fields, cleared your forests, built your railroads and cities, and brought forth treasures from the bowels of the earth, and helped make possible this magnificent representation of the progress of the South. Casting down your bucket among my people, helping and encouraging them as you are doing on these grounds, and to education of head, hand, and heart, you will find that they will buy your surplus land, make blossom the waste places in your fields, and run your factories. While doing this, you can be sure in the future, as in the past, that you and your families will be surrounded by the most patient, faithful, law-abiding, and unresentful people that the world has seen. As we have proved our loyalty to you in the past, in nursing your children, watching by the sickbed of your mothers and fathers, and often following them with tear-dimmed eyes to their graves, so in the future, in our humble way, we shall stand by you with a devotion that no foreigner can approach, ready to lay down our lives, if need be, in defense of yours, interlacing our industrial, commercial, civil, and religious life with yours in a way that shall make the interests of both races one. In all things that are purely social we can be as separate as the fingers, yet one as the hand in all things essential to mutual progress.

There is no defense or security for any of us except in the highest intelligence and development of all. If anywhere there are efforts tending to curtail the fullest growth of the Negro, let these efforts be turned into stimulating, encouraging, and making him the most useful and intelligent citizen. Effort or means so invested will pay a thousand percent interest. These efforts will be twice blessed—"blessing him that gives and him that takes."

There is no escape through law of man or God from the inevitable:

The laws of changeless justice bind
Oppressor with oppressed;
And close as sin and suffering joined
We march to fate abreast.

Nearly sixteen millions of hands will aid you in pulling the load upward; or they will pull against you the load downward. We shall constitute one-third and more of the ignorance and crime of the South, or one-third its intelligence and progress; we shall contribute one-third to the business and industrial prosperity of the South, or we shall prove a veritable body of death, stagnating, depressing, retarding every effort to advance the body politic. Gentlemen of the exposition, as we present to you our humble effort at an exhibition of our progress, you must not expect overmuch. Starting thirty years ago with ownership here and there in a few quilts and pumpkins and chickens (gathered from miscellaneous sources), remember the path that has led from these to the inventions and production of agricultural implements, buggies, steam engines, newspapers, books, statuary, carving, paintings, the management of drugstores and banks, has not been trodden without contact with thorns and thistles. While we take pride in what we exhibit as a result of our independent efforts, we do not for a moment forget that our part in this exhibition would fall far short of your expectations but for the constant help that has come to our educational life, not only from the Southern states, but especially from Northern philanthropists, who have made their gifts a constant stream of blessing and encouragement.

The wisest among my race understand that the agitation of questions of social equality is the extreme folly, and that progress in the enjoyment of all the privileges that will come to us must be the result of severe and constant struggle rather than of artificial forcing. No race that has anything to contribute to the markets of the world is long in any degree ostracized. It is important and right that all privileges of the law be ours, but it is vastly more important that we be prepared for the exercises of these privileges. The opportunity to earn a dollar in a factory just now is worth infinitely more than the opportunity to spend a dollar in an opera house.

In conclusion, may I repeat that nothing in thirty years has given us more hope and encouragement, and drawn us so near to you of the white race, as this opportunity offered by the exposition; and here bending, as it were, over the altar that represents the results of the struggles of your race and mine, both starting practically empty-handed three decades ago, I pledge that in your effort to work out the great and intricate problem which God has laid at the doors of the South, you shall have at all times the patient, sympathetic help of my race; only let this be constantly in mind, that, while from representations in these buildings of the product of field, of forest, of mine, of factory, letters, and art, much good will come, yet far above and beyond material benefits will be that higher good, that, let us pray God, will come, in a blotting out of sectional differences and racial animosities and suspicions, in a determination to administer absolute justice, in a willing obedience among all classes to the mandates of law. This, this, coupled with our material prosperity, will bring into our beloved South a new heaven and a new earth.

CROSS OF GOLD

This speech by William Jennings Bryan, delivered at the Democratic National Convention in Chicago on July 9, 1896, was quite probably the most effective oration in the history of American party politics. Bryan, then only thirty-six, had come to Chicago as a leader of the Nebraska delegation with the avowed intention of vaulting from this relatively obscure role into the presidential nomination. And that he did. The great issue before the convention was whether the party should take its place behind President Cleveland and the conservative Democrats in a continued defense of the gold standard or yield to the fervent demand of populists in the West for free coinage of silver—a remedy for depressed prices, unemployment, and the blight of depression. Bryan was perhaps the most articulate advocate of the silver strategy, which essentially called for the government to inflate the money supply. Though he was ultimately defeated by William McKinley in the general election, he had established himself as a political force to be contended with.

I would be presumptuous, indeed, to present myself against the distinguished gentlemen to whom you have listened if this were a mere measuring of abilities; but this is not a contest between persons. The humblest citizen in all the land, when clad in the armor of a righteous cause, is stronger than all the hosts of error. I come to speak to you in defense of a cause as holy as the cause of liberty—the cause of humanity.

When this debate is concluded, a motion will be made to lay upon the table the resolution offered in commendation of the administration, and also the resolution offered in condemnation of the administration. We object to bringing this question down to the level of persons. The individual is but an atom; he is born, he acts, he dies; but principles are eternal; and this has been a contest over a principle.

Never before in the history of this country has there been witnessed such a contest as that through which we have just passed. Never before in the history of American politics has a great issue been fought out as this issue has been, by the voters of a great party. On the fourth of March, 1895, a few Democrats, most of them members of Congress, issued an address to the Democrats of the nation, asserting that the money question was the paramount issue of the hour; declaring that a majority of the Democratic party had the right to control the action of the party on this paramount issue; and concluding with the request that the believers in the free coinage of silver in the Democratic party should organize, take charge of, and control the policy of the Democratic party. Three months later, at Memphis, an organization was perfected, and the silver Democrats went forth openly and courageously proclaiming their belief, and declaring that, if successful, they would crystallize into a platform the declaration which they had made. They began the conflict. With a zeal approaching the zeal which inspired the crusaders who followed Peter the Hermit, our silver Democrats went forth from victory unto victory until they are now assembled, not to discuss, not to debate, but to enter up the judgment already rendered by the plain people of this country. In this contest brother has been arrayed against brother, father against son. The warmest ties of love, acquaintance and association have been disregarded; old leaders have been cast aside when they have refused to give expression to the sentiments of those whom they would lead, and new leaders have sprung up to give direction to this cause of truth. Thus has the contest been waged, and we have assembled here under as binding and solemn instructions as were ever imposed upon representatives of the people.

We do not come as individuals. As individuals we might have been glad to compliment the gentleman from New York but we know that the people for whom we speak would never be willing to put him in a position where he could thwart the will of the Democratic party. I say it was not a question of persons; it was a question of principle, and it is not with gladness, my friends, that we find ourselves brought into conflict with those who are now arrayed on the other side.

The gentleman who preceded me spoke of the State of Massachusetts; let me assure him that not one present in all this convention entertains the least hostility to the people of the State of Massachusetts, but we stand here representing people who are the equals, before the law, of the greatest citizens in the State of Massachusetts. When you, turning to the gold delegates, come before us and tell us that we are about to disturb your business interests, we reply that you have disturbed our business interests by your course.

We say to you that you have made the definition of a business man too limited in its application. The man who is employed for wages is as much a business man as his employer; the attorney in a country town is as much a business man as the corporation counsel in a great metropolis; the merchant at the cross-roads store is as much a business man as the merchant of New York; the farmer who goes forth in the morning and toils all day—who begins in the spring and toils all summer—and who by the application of brain and muscle to the natural resources of the country creates wealth, is as much a business man as the man who goes upon the board of trade and bets upon the price of grain; the miners who go down a thousand feet into the earth, or climb two thousand feet upon the cliffs, and bring forth from their hiding places the precious metals to be poured into the channels of trade are as much business men as the few financial magnates who, in a back room, corner the money of the world. We come to speak for this broader class of business men.

Ah, my friends, we say not one word against those who live upon the Atlantic coast, but the hardy pioneers who have braved all the dangers of the wilderness, who have made the desert to blossom as the rose—the pioneers away out there who rear their children near to Nature's heart, where they can mingle their voices with the voices of the birds—out there where they have erected schoolhouses for the education of their young, churches where they praise their Creator, and cemeteries where rest the ashes of their dead—these people, we say, are as deserving of the consideration of our party as any people in this country. It is for these that we speak. We do not come as aggressors. Our war is not a war of conquest; we are fighting in the defense of our homes, our families, and posterity. We have petitioned, and our petitions have been scorned; we have entreated, and our entreaties have been disregarded; we have begged, and they have mocked when our calamity came. We beg no longer; we entreat no more; we petition no more. We defy them.

The gentleman from Wisconsin has said that he fears a Robespierre. My friends, in this land of the free you need not fear that a tyrant will spring up from among the people. What we need is an Andrew Jackson to stand, as Jackson stood, against the encroachments of organized wealth.

They tell us that this platform was made to catch votes. We reply to them that changing conditions make new issues; that the principles upon which Democracy rests are as everlasting as the hills, but that they must be applied to new conditions as they arise. Conditions have arisen, and we are here to meet those conditions. They tell us that the income tax ought not to be brought in here; that it is a new idea. They criticize us for our criticism of the Supreme Court of the United States. My friends, we have not criticized; we have simply called attention to what you already know. If you want criticisms, read the dissenting opinions of the court. There you will find criticisms. They say that we passed an unconstitutional law; we deny it. The income tax law was not unconstitutional when it was passed; it was not unconstitutional when it went before the Supreme Court for the first time; it did not become unconstitutional until one of the judges changed his mind, and we cannot be expected to know when a judge will change his mind. The income tax is just. It simply intends to put the burdens of government justly upon the backs of the people. I am in favor of an income tax. When I find a man who is not willing to bear his share of the burdens of the government which protects him, I find a man who is unworthy to enjoy the blessings of a government like ours.

They say that we are opposing national bank currency; that is true. If you will read what Thomas Benton said, you will find he said that, in searching history, he could find but one parallel to Andrew Jackson; that was Cicero, who destroyed the conspiracy of Cataline and saved Rome. Benton said that Cicero only did for Rome what Jackson did for us when he destroyed the bank conspiracy and saved America. We say in our platform that we believe that the right to coin and issue money is a function of government. We believe it. We believe that it is a part of sovereignty, and can no more with safety be delegated to private individuals than we could afford to delegate to private individuals the power to make penal statutes or levy taxes. Mr. Jefferson, who was once regarded as good Democratic authority, seems to have differed in opinion from the gentleman who has addressed us on the part of the minority. Those who are opposed to this proposition tell us that the issue of paper money is a function of the bank, and that the Government ought to go out of the banking business. I stand with Jefferson rather than with them, and tell them, as he did, that the issue of money is a function of government, and that the banks ought to go out of the governing business.

They complain about the plank which declares against life tenure in office. They have tried to strain it to mean that which it does not mean. What we oppose by that plank is the life tenure which is being built up in Washington, and which excludes from participation in official benefits the humbler members of society.

Let me call your attention to two or three important things. The gentleman from New York says that he will propose an amendment to the platform providing that the proposed change in our monetary system shall not affect contracts already made. Let me remind you that there is no intention of affecting those contracts which according to present laws are made payable in gold; but if he means to say that we cannot change our monetary system without protecting those who have loaned money before the change was made, I desire to ask him where, in law or in morals, he can find justification for not protecting the debtors when the act of 1873 was passed, if he now insists that we must protect the creditors.

He says he will also propose an amendment which will provide for the suspension of free coinage if we fail to maintain the party within a year. We reply that when we advocate a policy which we believe will be successful, we are not compelled to raise a doubt as to our own sincerity by suggesting what we shall do if we fail. I ask him, if he would apply his logic to us, why he does not apply it to himself. He says he wants this country to try to secure an international agreement. Why does he not tell us what he is going to do if he fails to secure an international agreement? There is more reason for him to do that than there is for us to provide against the failure to maintain the parity. Our opponents have tried for twenty years to secure an international agreement, and those are waiting for it most patiently who do not want it at all.

And now, my friends, let me come to the paramount issue. If they ask us why it is that we say more on the money question than we say upon the tariff question, I reply that, if protection has slain its thousands, the gold standard has slain its tens of thousands. If they ask us why we do not embody in our platform all the things that we believe in, we reply that when we have restored the money of the Constitution all other necessary reforms will be possible; but that until this is done there is no other reform that can be accomplished.

Why is it that within three months such a change has come over the country? Three months ago, when it was confidently asserted that those who believe in the gold standard would frame our platform and nominate our candidates, even the advocates of the gold standard did not think that we could elect a president. And they had good reason for their doubt, because there is scarcely a State here today asking for the gold standard which is not in the absolute control of the Republican party. But note the change. Mr. McKinley was nominated at St. Louis upon a platform which declared for the maintenance of the gold standard until it can be changed into bimetallism by international agreement. Mr. McKinley was the most popular man among the Republicans, and three months ago everybody in the Republican party prophesied his election. How is it today? Why, the man who was once pleased to think that he looked like Napoleon—that man shudders today when he remembers that he was nominated on the anniversary of the battle of Waterloo. Not only that, but as he listens he can hear with ever-increasing distinctness the sound of the waves as they beat upon the lonely shores of St. Helena.

Why this change? Ah, my friends, is not the reason for the change evident to any one who will look at the matter? No private character, however pure, no personal popularity, however great, can protect from the avenging wrath of an indignant people a man who will declare that he is in favor of fastening the gold standard upon this country, or who is willing to surrender the right of self-government and place the legislative control of our affairs in the hands of foreign potentates and powers.

We go forth confident that we shall win. Why? Because upon the paramount issue of this campaign there is not a spot of ground upon which the enemy will dare to challenge battle. If they tell us that the gold standard is a good thing, we shall point to their platform and tell them that their platform pledges the party to get rid of the gold standard and substitute bimetallism. If the gold standard is a good thing, why try to get rid of it? I call your attention to the fact that some of the very people who are in this convention today and who tell us that we ought to declare in favor of international bimetallism—thereby declaring that the gold standard is wrong and that the principle of bimetallism is better—these very people four months ago were open and avowed advocates of the gold standard, and were then telling us that we could not legislate two metals together, even with the aid of all the world. If the gold standard is a good thing, we ought to declare in favor of its retention and not in favor of abandoning it; and if the gold standard is a bad thing why should we wait until other nations are willing to help us to let go? Here is the line of battle, and we care not upon which issue they force the fight; we are prepared to meet them on either issue or on both. If they tell us that the gold standard is the standard of civilization, we reply to them that this, the most enlightened of all the nations of the earth, has never declared for a gold standard and that both the great parties this year are declaring against it. If the gold standard is the standard of civilization, why, my friends, should we not have it? If they come to meet us on that issue we can present the history of our nation. More than that; we can tell them that they will search the pages of history in vain to find a single instance where the common people of any land have ever declared themselves in favor of the gold standard. They can find where the holders of the fixed investments have declared for a gold standard, but not where the masses have.

Mr. Carlisle said in 1878 that this was a struggle between "the idle holders of idle capital" and "the struggling masses, who produce the wealth and pay the taxes of the country"; and, my friends, the question we are to decide is: Upon which side will the Democratic party fight; upon the side of "the idle holders of idle capital" or upon the side of "the struggling masses"? That is the question which the party must answer first, and then it must be answered by each individual hereafter. The sympathies of the Democratic party, as shown by the platform, are on the side of the struggling masses who have ever been the foundation of the Democratic party. There are two ideas of government. There are those who believe that if you will only legislate to make the well-to-do prosperous, their prosperity will leak through on those below. The Democratic idea, however, has been that if you legislate to make the masses prosperous, their prosperity will find its way up through every class which rests upon them.

You come to us and tell us that the great cities are in favor of the gold standard; we reply that the great cities rest upon our broad and fertile prairies. Burn down your cities and leave our farms, and your cities will spring up again as if by magic; but destroy our farms and the grass will grow in the streets of every city in the country.

My friends, we declare that this nation is able to legislate for its own people on every question, without waiting for the aid or consent of any other nation on earth; and upon that issue we expect to carry every State in the Union. I shall not slander the inhabitants of the fair State of Massachusetts nor the inhabitants of the State of New York by saying that, when they are confronted with the proposition, they will declare that this nation is not able to attend to its own business. It is the issue of 1776 over again. Our ancestors, when but three millions in number, had the courage to declare their political independence of every other nation; shall we, their descendants, when we have grown to seventy millions, declare that we are less independent than our forefathers? No, my friends, that will never be the verdict of our people. Therefore, we care not upon what lines the battle is fought. If they say bimetallism is good, but that we cannot have it until other nations help us, we reply that, instead of having a gold standard because England has, we will restore bimetallism, and then let England have bimetallism because the United States has it. If they dare to come out in the open field and defend the gold standard as a good thing, we will fight them to the uttermost. Having behind us the producing masses of this nation and the world, supported by the commercial interests, the laboring interests, and the toilers everywhere, we will answer their demand for a gold standard by saying to them: You shall not press down upon the brow of labor this crown of thorns, you shall not crucify mankind upon a cross of gold.

THE NEW COLOSSUS

*Written in 1883, this poem by Emma Lazarus gained fame
after it was inscribed on the Statue of Liberty in 1903. Thereafter, it became a kind of beacon light of hope to the oppressed
peoples of the world. To this day it conveys the exceptionalism of
the American experiment in national life—one that is rooted
first and foremost in a set of ideas about freedom.*

Not like the brazen giant of Greek fame,
With conquering limbs astride from land to land;
Here at our sea-washed, sunset gates shall stand
A mighty woman with a torch, whose flame
Is the imprisoned lightning, and her name
Mother of Exiles. From her beacon-hand
Glows worldwide welcome; her mild eyes command
The air-bridged harbor that twin cities frame.

"Keep, ancient lands, your storied pomp!" cries she
With silent lips. "Give me your tired, your poor,
Your huddled masses yearning to breathe free,
The wretched refuse of your teeming shore.
Send these, the homeless, tempest-tost to me,
I lift my lamp beside the golden door!"

THE MAN WITH THE MUCK-RAKE

One of the most popular men who ever held the highest political office in the land, Theodore Roosevelt made his reputation as a reformer. His entire career was a kind of crusade against systemic corruption and injustice. Unlike most reformers, however, he was profoundly committed to conservative principles; his reforms were designed to preserve the heritage of Christendom rather than to merely innovate. That unique combination of progressivism and conservatism is especially evident in this speech, which he delivered to the House of Representatives on April 14, 1906.

Over a century ago Washington laid the cornerstone of the Capitol in what was then little more than a tract of wooded wilderness here beside the Potomac. We now find it necessary to provide by great additional buildings for the business of the government. This growth in the need for the housing of the government is but a proof and example of the way in which the nation has grown and the sphere of action of the national government has grown. We now administer the affairs of a nation in which the extraordinary growth of population has been outstripped by the growth of wealth and the growth in complex interests. The material problems that face us today are not such as they were in Washington's time, but the underlying facts of human nature are the same now as they were then. Under altered external form we war with the same tendencies toward evil that were evident in Washington's time, and are helped by the same tendencies for good. It is about some of these that I wish to say a word today.

In Bunyan's *Pilgrim's Progress* you may recall the description of the Man with the Muck-rake, the man who could look no way but downward, with the muck-rake in his hand; who was offered a celestial crown for his muck-rake, but who would neither look up nor regard the crown he was offered, but continued to rake to himself the filth of the floor.

In *Pilgrim's Progress* the Man with the Muck-rake is set forth as the example of him whose vision is fixed on carnal instead of on spiritual things. Yet he also typifies the man who in this life consistently refuses to see aught that is lofty and fixes his eyes with solemn intentness only on that which is vile and debasing. Now, it is very necessary that we should not flinch from seeing what is vile and debasing. There is filth on the floor, and it must be scraped up with the muck-rake: and there are times and places where this service is the most needed of all the services that can be performed. But the man who never does anything else, who never thinks or speaks or writes save of his feats with the muck-rake, speedily becomes, not a help to society, not an incitement to good, but one of the most potent forces for evil.

There are, in the body politic, economic, and social, many and grave evils, and there is urgent necessity for the sternest war upon them. There should be relentless exposure of and attack upon every evil man, whether politician or business man, every evil practice, whether in politics, in business, or in social life. I hail as a benefactor every writer or speaker, every man who, on the platform, or in book, magazine, or newspaper, with merciless severity makes such attack, provided always that he in his turn remembers that the attack is of use only if it is absolutely truthful. The liar is no whit better than the thief, and if his mendacity takes the form of slander, he may be worse than most thieves. It puts a premium upon knavery untruthfully to attack an honest man, or even with hysterical exaggeration to assail a bad man with untruth. An epidemic of indiscriminate assault upon character does no good but very great harm.

My plea is not for immunity to, but for the most unsparing exposure of the politician who betrays his trust, of the big-business man who makes or spends his fortune in illegitimate or corrupt ways. There should be a resolute effort to hunt every such man out of the position he has disgraced. Expose the crime, and hunt down the criminal; but remember that even in the case of crime, if it is attacked in sensational, lurid, and untruthful fashion, the attack may do more damage to the public mind than the crime itself. It is because I feel that there should be no rest in the endless war against the forces of evil that I ask that the war be conducted with sanity as well as with resolution. The men with the muck-rakes are often indispensable to the well-being of society; but only if they know when to stop raking the muck, and to look upward to the celestial crown above them, to the crown of worthy endeavor. There are beautiful things above and round about them; and if they gradually grow to feel that the whole world is nothing but muck, their power of usefulness is gone. If the whole picture is painted black, there remains no hue whereby to single out the rascals for distinction from their fellows. Such painting finally induces a kind of moral colorblindness; and people affected by it come to the conclusion that no man is really black, and no man really white, but that all are gray.

To assail the great and admitted evils of our political and industrial life with such crude and sweeping general-izations as to include decent men in the general condem-nation means the searing of the public conscience. There results a general attitude either of cynical belief in and indifference to public corruption or else of a distrustful inability to discriminate between the good and the bad. Either attitude is fraught with untold damage to the coun-try as a whole. The fool who has not sense to discriminate between what is good and what is bad is well-nigh as dan-gerous as the man who does discriminate and yet chooses the bad. There is nothing more distressing to every good patriot, to every good American, than the hard, scoffing spirit which treats the allegation of dishonesty in a public man as a cause for laughter.

There is any amount of good in the world, and there never was a time when loftier and more disinterested work for the betterment of mankind was being done than now.

The forces that tend for evil are great and terrible but the forces of truth and love and courage and honesty and generosity and sympathy are also stronger than ever before. It is a foolish and timid, no less than a wicked, thing to blink the fact that the forces of evil are strong, but it is even worse to fail to take into account the strength of the forces that tell for good. Hysterical sensationalism is the very poorest weapon wherewith to fight for lasting righteousness. The men who, with stern sobriety and truth, assail the many evils of our time, whether in the public press, or in magazines, or in books, are the leaders and allies of all engaged in the work for social and political betterment. But if they give good reason for distrust of what they say, if they chill the ardor of those who demand truth as a primary virtue, they thereby betray the good cause, and play into the hands of the very men against whom they are nominally at war.

We can no more and no less afford to condone evil in the man of capital than evil in the man of no capital. The wealthy man who exults because there is a failure of justice in the effort to bring some trust magnate to an account for his misdeeds is as bad as, and no worse than, the so-called labor leader who clamorously strives to excite a foul class feeling on behalf of some other labor leader who is implicated in murder. One attitude is as bad as the other and no worse; in each case the accused is entitled to exact justice; and in neither case is there need of action by others which can be construed into an expression of sympathy for crime.

There is nothing more antisocial in a democratic republic like ours than such vicious class-consciousness.

It is important to this people to grapple with the problems connected with the amassing of enormous fortunes, and the use of those fortunes, both corporate and individual, in business. We should discriminate in the sharpest way between fortunes well won and fortunes ill won; between those gained as an incident to performing great services to the community as a whole, and those gained in evil fashion by keeping just within the limits of mere law-honesty. Of course no amount of charity in spending such fortunes in any way compensates for misconduct in making them. As a matter of personal conviction, and without pretending to discuss the details or formulate the system, I feel that we shall ultimately have to consider the adoption of some such scheme as that of a progressive tax on all fortunes, beyond a certain amount, either given in life or devised or bequeathed upon death to any individual—a tax so framed as to put it out of the power of the owner of one of these enormous fortunes to hand on more than a certain amount to any one individual.

The eighth commandment reads "Thou shalt not steal." It does not read "Thou shalt not steal from the rich man." It does not read "Thou shalt not steal from the poor man." It reads, simply and plainly, "Thou shalt not steal." No good whatever will come from that warped and mock morality which denounces the misdeeds of men of wealth and forgets the misdeeds practiced at their expense; which denounces bribery, but blinds itself to blackmail; which foams with rage if a corporation secures favors by improper methods, and merely leers with hideous mirth if the corporation is itself wronged. The only public servant who can be trusted honestly to protect the rights of the public against the misdeeds of a corporation is that public man who will just as surely protect the corporation itself from wrongful aggression. If a public man is willing to yield to popular clamor and do wrong to the men of wealth or to rich corporations, it may be set down as certain that if the opportunity comes he will secretly and furtively do wrong to the public in the interest of a corporation.

More important than aught else is the development of the broadest sympathy of man for man. The welfare of the wage-worker, the welfare of the tiller of the soil—upon this depends the welfare of the entire country; their good is not to be sought in pulling down others; but their good must be the prime object of all our statesmanship.

Materially we must strive to secure a broader economic opportunity for all men, so that each shall have a better chance to show the stuff of which he is made. Spiritually and ethically we must strive to bring about clean living and right thinking. We appreciate that the things of the body are important; but we appreciate also that the things of the soul are immeasurably more important. The foundation stone of national life is, and ever must be, the high individual character of the average citizen.

VICTORY BELLS

The Great War, known later as the First World War, was the most brutal and devastating war the civilized world had ever witnessed up to this point. As a result, when peace finally came in 1918, there was much rejoicing on both sides of the battle lines. This poem by Grace Conkling, set to a popular jazz tune, highlighted the exultant relief of a world once again at peace.

I heard the bells across the trees,
I heard them ride the plunging breeze
Above the roofs from tower and spire,
And they were leaping like a fire,
And they were shining like a stream
With sun to make its music gleam.
Deep tones as though the thunder tolled,
Cool voices thin as tinkling gold,
They shook the spangled autumn down
From out the tree-tops of the town;
They left great furrows in the air
And made a clangor everywhere
As of metallic wings. They flew
Aloft in spirals to the blue
Tall tent of heaven and disappeared.

And others, swift as though they feared
The people might not heed their cry
Went shouting "victory up" the sky.
They did not say that war is done,
Only that glory has begun
Like sunrise, and the coming day
Will burn the clouds of war away.
There will be time for dreams again,
And home-coming for weary men.

THE LIVES OF THE PRESIDENTS

Once the Constitution was ratified, the office of the presidency took on a whole new importance. The men who served in that office just after the Founding Era up to the advent of modernity had the awesome task of directing the gangling young American republic toward its manifest destiny. Sadly, that task was disrupted by innumerable conflicts including a terrible civil war in the 1860s, a bitter struggle for universal franchise in the 1960s, and two world wars in between. The stories of the men who led the nation during the intervening years reflect both the tenacity and the fragility of this great experiment in liberty.

GEORGE WASHINGTON (1732–99)

To Gen. George Washington fell the unprecedented task of organizing a national administration that was somehow to govern the thirteen separate states and yet preserve the freedoms for which the independent men of these states had so recently fought. It was his extraordinary task to make the radical idea of a government of freemen, by freemen, actually work, with nothing but the noble words of the freshly written Constitution to guide him. There were no existing buildings or departments, no procedures, precedents, or traditions; there was no capitol. There was simply the Constitution and the man—and the mighty task. Like other colonial landholders, Washington was a new kind of man in history—part cultivated gentleman, part rugged pioneer, a man in whom the ideas of Western civilization were combined with the great physical strength and fierce spirit of independence of the frontiersman. Among such men, Washington was outstanding. His performance as a surveyor and a soldier on the western frontier earned him, at twenty-three, the command of Virginia's troops, and he served in the House of Burgesses for years before the Continental Congress chose him to lead the Continental Army. As its commander he held the struggling patriots together during the long war years; with victory, he quietly retired from the field. The presidential electors from the nearly sovereign states, cautious in selecting the man to hold power over all the states, had little to fear from one who had so willingly relinquished control of a victorious army. Already one of the country's leading citizens, Washington carried out his duties as president with simple dignity. Although he tried to remain free of parties, he was closer to the Federalist Hamilton, his secretary of the treasury, than to the Democrat Jefferson, his secretary of state. He firmly declined a third term, and spent his last years peacefully at his beautiful plantation, Mount Vernon, where his tomb now stands. Of all memorials, the most dramatic is the graceful shaft of the monument in the District of Columbia which symbolizes the aspirations of America as they were so nobly embodied in the undoubted "father of our country."

JOHN ADAMS (1735–1826)

It was natural that Washington's vice president, Adams, should succeed Washington, for in his own contentious but courageous way, he had contributed much to the new nation. Unlike Washington, Adams was not a great leader: he had neither a commanding nor a magnetic personality; he was a lawyer and an intellectual who made his greatest contributions before he became president. A man of bristling integrity, he could devote himself to a cause with a fierce intensity: he condemned the Stamp Act of 1765, was one of the first to support the idea of independence, and, at the Continental Congress when the colonies wavered before the mighty decision, he vigorously fought for acceptance of the Declaration of Independence. He further distinguished himself by representing the infant country with dignity—and success—in the leading courts of Europe. By 1789 Adams was a respected but not a popular figure. In finishing second to Washington he barely received enough votes to secure the vice presidency—and for eight years he was continually in the shadow of the commanding figure of Washington. Unfortunately his own term was little better. His struggle with Alexander Hamilton and his cabinet members created factional strife in both the Federalist Party and the government. Through the bitter disputes Adams remained essentially a Federalist, maintaining the strong central government established by Washington and Hamilton. When the Federalists passed the oppressive Alien and Sedition Laws in 1789, they assumed such sweeping powers over all critics of government that they challenged the essential freedoms of the individual; the party, already too closely allied with the propertied colonial aristocracy, carried the idea of a strong central government too far. Both Adams and the party lost favor: in the 1800 election Adams was defeated by Jefferson and the new Republican Party. Interestingly, Jefferson and Adams—once fierce rivals—became close friends in their elder years. They even died on the same day, within hours of one another—on July 4, 1826.

THOMAS JEFFERSON (1743–1826)

Called the "Bloodless Revolution of 1800," Jefferson's election marked a profound but peaceful change in the administration of the young nation. The revolutionist who boldly wrote religious and ethical beliefs into the Declaration of Independence brought to the presidency a philosophy of government firmly rooted in those same beliefs, a philosophy that concerned itself, above all, with the rights and liberties of the individual. It was Jefferson's democratic views, with his enduring faith in the individual, that, more than anything else, turned the country away from the class rule of the Federalists. Few men have been better equipped to become president—a graduate of William and Mary College and an able lawyer, Jefferson helped shape the destiny of the struggling nation from the beginning. He served in the Virginia House of Burgesses, in the Continental Congress—writing the final draft of the Declaration, as a minister in the French court; as governor of Virginia, as secretary of state under Washington, and vice president under Adams. But as president, Jefferson proved that philosophic ability and experience in office were no replacements for political leadership. He was a remarkable inventor, a scientist, a writer, an artist, a planter, an architect, a musician, and an educator—but he was a poor politician and administrator. He was able, however, to bring a profound sense of democracy to the nation's highest office, an accomplishment that ranks with the celebrated purchase of the Louisiana Territory as an outstanding achievement of his administration. A complex, brilliant man, Jefferson was one of the most accomplished of our presidents—he was talented as are few men in any age—the living example of his own abiding belief in the capacity of the individual to learn and to grow under freedom.

JAMES MADISON (1751–1836)

A devoted disciple of Jefferson, Madison became the active leader of the Democratic-Republican Party when he was elected president. And like his mentor, he was never able to provide the kind of administrative leadership necessary to guide the nation. Like John Adams, Madison performed his greatest service to the nation before he was elected president. Increasingly aware of the

weaknesses of the confederation that loosely bound the
states after the Revolution, he helped frame the Constitution in the Convention of 1787 and eloquently
defended it in the Virginia Ratifying Convention and in
the famed Federalist Papers. And after the new government was formed, it was Madison who introduced the
Bill of Rights to Congress as the first amendments to the
Constitution. The smallest man ever to become president, the soft-spoken, retiring Madison was more a
scholar than an executive. He developed the habit of serious study at the College of New Jersey—under the tute-
lage of John Witherspoon—and became a devoted
student of history and law. Besides the Constitution and
the Federalist Papers, other documents that helped shape
the new nation can be traced to his pen: the petition for
religious freedom in Virginia, the defense of American
navigation rights on the Mississippi, and the Virginia
Resolution—a ringing denouncement of the oppressive
Alien and Sedition Laws. Foreign problems dominated
Madison's years as president. Conflict with Britain over
naval rights finally led to a war that brought little credit
to either nation and made Madison the most unpopular
president the country had thus far known. Federalists
demanded that he resign, but he weathered the criticism;
with peace he regained a measure of popularity. But
nothing that he accomplished as president—or as
member of Congress or secretary of state—won him the
high place he had already gained as one of the Founders

of the nation, a place of enduring fame as the Father of the Constitution.

JAMES MONROE (1758–1831)

The first extended period of peace came to the young nation with Monroe's administration, the serene years known as the Era of Good Feeling. The European nations, exhausted by the Napoleonic wars, let the new nation develop in peace, and Monroe—and the United States—made the most of it: the United States persuaded Britain to agree to disarm forever along the Canadian border, purchased Florida from Spain, and asserted its growing authority by proclaiming the Monroe Doctrine—the warning to European nations against further conquest or colonization in the Western Hemisphere. At home the problem of slavery was temporarily solved by the Missouri Compromise, which admitted Missouri as a slave state but prohibited slavery north of the Mason-Dixon Line. Before reaching the presidency, Monroe served in a variety of posts: he began as an eighteen-year-old lieutenant in the Revolution; forty years later he held the unusual cabinet position of secretary of state and war. His long career was punctuated with controversy: as Washington's minister to France he earned Federalist disapproval and, finally, removal by his sympathy for the French cause; as Jefferson's minister to England, he concluded a treaty on naval problems that failed to uphold American rights and was, therefore, rejected by Jefferson.

However, as Jefferson's minister extraordinaire in France he won a share of the credit for the purchase of Louisiana by signing the treaty that concluded the greatest of real estate transactions. Monroe's administration brought to an end almost a quarter century of rule by the close friends that the Federalists called the Virginia Dynasty—Jefferson, Madison, and Monroe. Like his friends, Monroe almost exhausted his fortune in a lifetime of public service; with them he helped block the Federalists' drift toward class rule and furthered the establishment of the government according to Jeffersonian principles of democracy.

JOHN QUINCY ADAMS (1767–1848)

Monroe was the last of the Southern aristocrats of the Virginia Dynasty. The man who succeeded him was the last of the Northern aristocrats of the Massachusetts Dynasty—the Adams family of Braintree. For Adams, although not born to the purple, was born to the red, white, and blue. He literally grew up with the country—as a boy he watched the battle of Bunker Hill from a hill near home; at fourteen he served as secretary to the minister to Russia; at sixteen secretary at the treaty ending the Revolution; and he later held more offices than any earlier president. The only son of a president ever to reach that office, Adams followed a career that closely resembled his father's—both attended Harvard, studied law, and were successful ministers and peace commissioners in Europe; both were elected president for only one term; both became involved in party conflicts and spent their least successful years in the White House. Studious and crotchety, Adams was more successful as a diplomat and statesman than as a politician. As Monroe's secretary of state he negotiated with the Spanish for Florida and was largely responsible for the document that became known as the Monroe Doctrine. In the unusual election of 1824, four Democrat-Republicans contended for the presidency. Andrew Jackson received almost 50,000 votes more than Adams, but less than the required majority. The decision thus rested with the House of Representatives, and when Henry Clay threw his support to Adams, the House elected Adams. Jackson felt cheated. The strong feeling that developed between Jackson and Adams ruined Adams's administration and finally drove the two men into separate parties—Adams the National Republicans, Jackson the Democrats. Adams was more successful in Congress, where he served for his last seventeen years. There he distinguished himself by his dedicated fight to remove the "gag rule," which prevented Congress from considering any antislavery petitions. After fourteen years of struggle he finally won. But his service did not end until he collapsed on the floor of Congress in 1848, sixty-six years after he first served his country at his father's side.

ANDREW JACKSON (1767–1845)

The first man of the people to become president; Jackson's election in 1828 stands in American history as a great divide between government by aristocrats—the rich and well-born, as Hamilton described them—and government by leaders who were drawn from, and identified themselves with, the people. Under Jackson, Jefferson's democratic principles became more of a political reality, but Jackson had to reconcile those principles of political equality with the economic problems of an expanding industrial economy in a growing country. His election, like Jefferson's, marked a revolution in American democracy. A child of the western frontier, Jackson was as rough-hewn as the log walls of his birthplace. From the time, at fourteen, when he fought in the Revolution, his life was largely one of struggle. On the frontier he studied law and gradually rose in Tennessee politics, representing the new state in Congress before he became state supreme court judge. But he gained fame not as a politician, but as a military hero. In the War of 1812 he commanded the American forces that roundly defeated the British at New Orleans. Tall, with a commanding presence, Jackson had a large, devoted personal following. And his stunning victory over John Quincy Adams in 1828 helped convince him that he was the champion of the people. With such a mandate he exercised his authority with a firm, and sometimes reckless, hand: he asserted the supremacy of the federal government when South Carolina tried to nullify tariff laws, and, in his most dramatic act, he boldly vetoed the recharter of the Bank of the United States, the half-private bank that had become powerful enough to threaten the government itself. Jackson proclaimed that the government should not "make the rich richer and the potent more powerful" at the expense of the rest of society. The man who had been elected by a great popular majority—and had himself risen from the people—proved thirty years before Lincoln that American democracy could achieve government not only of and for the people, but by the people as well.

MARTIN VAN BUREN (1782–1862)

Martin Van Buren was America's first political boss. Elegant in dress, amiable and courteous in manner, "Little Van" early demonstrated such political skill that he rapidly rose to prominence in New York state politics: he became one of the leaders of the "Albany Regency," a political machine that developed a spoils system on a large scale and gained control of state politics in the 1820s. A masterful organizer, he welded diverse regional interests into the first effective national political party—the new Democrat Party, which, in 1828, supported Andrew Jackson for the presidency. Coming to the presidency after the fiery general, Van Buren inherited thorny financial problems; shortly after he took office, there were bread riots and banks failed—the country was caught up in the Panic of 1837. The skilled politician who had earned such names as "The Little Magician" and "The American Talleyrand" was unable to avert the financial upheaval, but he courageously attempted to improve matters. He established what later became the Treasury Department, independent of any bank. But his administration was generally held responsible for the Panic. He never regained his earlier popularity and was defeated by William Harrison in 1840. No more was the charming little gentleman in a snuff-colored coat seen gliding through the streets of Washington in an elegantly fitted coach attended by liveried footmen. Although he remained a national figure for many years, and was an unsuccessful presidential candidate for the Free Soil Party in 1848, he spent most of his time in retirement at Lindenwald, his estate at Kinderhook, the quiet little village on the Hudson where he was born.

WILLIAM H. HARRISON (1773–1841)

In 1840 the Whigs took the gamble of nominating the oldest man ever to run for president, sixty-eight-year-old William H. Harrison, and they won the election but lost the gamble, for Harrison lived only one month after his inauguration—he had made a three-hour inaugural speech in a drenching rain and caught pneumonia. He served the shortest term of any president, but his election ended the Jacksonian reign and brought the growing Whigs to power, even though John Tyler, the vice president who succeeded Harrison, was a former Democrat with rather watery Whig convictions. The election of 1840 marked the beginning of elaborate national campaigns—by then the Whigs had become established as a second party, a development that helped to institutionalize the party system as the country's method of selecting candidates. Smarting from their defeat in 1836, when they were new and poorly organized, the Whigs met almost a year before the election for their first national convention. They then proceeded to build an elaborate campaign around everything but the issues: Harrison's military exploits against the Indians—especially the battle of Tippecanoe; and his service as a simple man of the West—the Ohio and Indiana Territories where he served as a civil and military leader. Campaign posters pictured Harrison as "The Hero of Tippecanoe" or "The Farmer of North Bend," hand to the plow in front of a log cabin. The catchy slogan "Tippecanoe and Tyler, too" rang out at the largest political rallies and mass meetings ever held in America. And it is one of the ironies of politics that the log cabin developed into a potent campaign symbol for Harrison, a man who was born in a white-pillared mansion into one of the aristocratic families of Tidewater Virginia. His father, Benjamin Harrison, was one of the Founding Fathers of the nation, a member of the Continental Congress, and a signer of the Declaration of Independence.

JOHN TYLER (1790–1862)

A tall Virginia gentleman, Tyler was the first vice president to complete the unexpired term of a president, but it is almost certain that the Whigs would never have chosen him as their vice presidential candidate had they known he was to serve all but a month of Harrison's term. For by 1840 "Honest John" had clearly demonstrated that he was not a party man: during his years in Washington as a nominally Democratic congressman and senator he had followed such an independent course—fighting the Missouri Compromise, fighting high tariffs, fighting Jackson—that it finally led him, by 1833, out of the Democratic Party altogether; yet his views on states' rights and on strict construction of the Constitution would never permit him to be at home with the Whigs. But the Whigs had nominated him, and, after Harrison's death, they had to live with him—as their chief executive. It is not surprising that Tyler's years in the White House were tempestuous ones. When his stand on states' rights led him to veto a bill for a Bank of the United States, every member of Harrison's original cabinet except Webster promptly resigned, and Webster, as secretary of state, was at the time deeply involved in settling the northeastern boundary dispute with Great Britain. Tyler further alienated the Whigs by repudiating the spoils system and refusing to replace some Democratic ministers abroad. Throughout his term he was unable to work in harmony with the Whig majority in Congress, who were led by Henry Clay, the actual political leader of the party. They did agree with Tyler, however, on the annexation of Texas, which was accomplished in the final days of Tyler's term. But in the election of 1844 only an irregular Democratic convention nominated Tyler, and he withdrew before election. At a time when political parties were emerging as powers on the national political scene, John Tyler left the White House, a president without a party. He served in the Confederate Congress at the end of his life, and was a strong supporter of Southern nullification and secession.

JAMES K. POLK (1795–1849)

An expansionist mood dominated the country in the mid-1840s and the man who caught the spirit of the times and came from nowhere to lead the country through the period of its greatest expansion was the Tennessean, Polk. In spite of this distinction, Polk has been one of the most neglected of our presidents. Emerging from comparative oblivion to become president, he has somehow managed to return there—in spite of a successful administration, one called by several leading historians "the one bright spot in the dull void between Jackson and Lincoln." When the delegates to the Democratic convention met in Baltimore in 1844, Polk was not even considered for the presidency; before the convention was over he had become the first dark-horse candidate. And, in the election, when the Whigs made "Who Is Polk?" their battle cry, he answered them by soundly defeating their candidate Henry Clay, who was running in his third presidential race. As president the little-known Polk was a strong, although not radical, expansionist. During his administration the nation acquired the vast lands in the Southwest and Far West that extended the borders of the country almost to the present continental limits. He proved to be a forceful president in his direction of the Mexican War and in settling the Oregon boundary dispute with Great Britain; yet he did not yield to the extremists who wanted all of Mexico, nor to those who cried "Fifty-four forty or fight!" and claimed the Oregon Territory clear to the Alaskan border. But the man who successfully led the country through its period of expansion strangely faded away when his work was done. Still popular at the end of his term but exhausted from overwork, Polk declined to be a candidate and returned to his home in Nashville, where he died only three months after leaving the White House—at the age of fifty-three.

ZACHARY TAYLOR (1784–1850)

Tobacco-chewing Gen. Zachary Taylor was the first regular army man to become president. It was solely on the strength of his popularity as a military hero that the Whigs chose him in 1848; never had a candidate known less about government, law, or politics. "Old Rough and Ready" had practically no formal education, had spent his entire life moving from one army post to another, and had never voted in an election in his life. Although earlier presidents had distinguished themselves in military service, none had made the regular army a career as Taylor did. Commissioned a first lieutenant in the infantry in 1808, he served in almost every war and skirmish for the next forty years. As a young captain in the War of 1812 he showed himself a cool and courageous leader; he won further recognition in the wars with the Black Hawks and Seminoles in later years. But it was his dramatic success in leading the American forces against the Mexican army in 1846–47 that caught the imagination of the American people and made him a national hero. In battle after battle he defeated the Mexicans—at Palo Alto, Reseca de la Palma, and Monterrey—and then on February 22, 1847, he won his greatest victory at Buena Vista when his troops routed a large army led by Gen. Santa Anna. In the White House, Taylor saw his job as the civilian counterpart of a military commander; untutored in politics, he tried to remain nonpartisan, to leave legislative matters to Congress and simply execute the laws himself. But running the government proved more complex: before long he became embroiled in the issue that haunted the country—slavery. Although unskilled in politics, he was a forthright and determined leader: when Southern congressmen threatened trouble over the admission of California as a free state, Taylor, who owned slaves himself, warned that he would lead the army against them and hang any who resisted as traitors. Thus the hero of the Mexican War, who died unexpectedly in July 1850, proved that, for all his lack of skill, he yet was able to take a stand on the issue the country dreaded facing. No successor until Lincoln was to show such courage.

MILLARD FILLMORE (1800–1874)

When Vice President Fillmore succeeded to the presidency upon the death of Zachary Taylor, he became one of the select group of presidents who have made the American myth "from a log cabin to the White House" a reality. But Fillmore's rise from humble apprentice to the highest office in the land was more inspiring than his performance in that office. When the short, stocky Taylor was still in the White House, Washingtonians observed that the tall, dignified Fillmore looked more like a president than the president himself. Born in a log cabin in Cayuga County, New York, Fillmore overcame extreme handicaps—he had little formal education, worked on his father's farm, and at fifteen was apprenticed to a wool carder. While serving his apprenticeship he belatedly began his studies and gradually learned enough to teach school himself, so that he could afford to study law. At twenty-three he was admitted to the bar; by the time he was thirty he had established himself in Buffalo and won a seat in the New York State Assembly. In politics Fillmore generally followed a moderate course, although in Congress he did espouse an unpopular cause by supporting John Quincy Adams in his fight against the "gag rule" against antislavery bills. But as president he accepted Henry Clay's compromise measures on slavery and signed his political life away when he signed the Fugitive Slave Act. Part of the Compromise of 1850, the act permitted slave owners to seize Negroes in the North as fugitives without process of law. The act aroused extreme bitterness in the North; instead of improving conditions, it drove North and South ever farther apart. Although Fillmore could not then have realized it, his political career was practically over. The man who looked the part of a president was not even nominated by his own party to play the role again—although he continued to be a third-party threat for nearly another quarter century.

FRANKLIN PIERCE (1804–69)

"I would rather be right than President," Henry Clay said, and he was often right but never president. But Franklin Pierce, a genial New Hampshire lawyer who said that the presidency would be "utterly repugnant" to him, became president in spite of himself—without ever making a single campaign speech. Like Polk, Pierce had not even been considered a candidate before the Democratic convention, but he was reluctantly pushed into the role of compromise candidate when the convention reached a stalemate at the thirty-fifth ballot. Although he served honorably in his state legislature and in the House and Senate, Pierce gradually developed a marked distaste for politics—in 1842 he resigned from the Senate to return to private practice, and later he refused several opportunities to return to office. Handsome, friendly Pierce had retired from politics for life until he was caught up in the swirl of events that suddenly put him in the White House. In 1853 slavery was still a dominating issue. Pierce took office with the belief that he should support the Compromise of 1850, and like Fillmore, he alienated the North by enforcing the Fugitive Slave Act. The Kansas-Nebraska Act, which created new territories in 1854, simply provided a new arena for the great struggle. In these new territories nothing was settled as abolitionists and pro-slavery groups resorted to force and bloodshed: "Bleeding Kansas" became an open wound. On other fronts Pierce fared little better. Part of his expansionist policy was a plan to purchase Cuba, but he was forced to denounce three of his ministers—one of them was his successor, James Buchanan—when they declared in the Ostend Manifesto that America should take Cuba, if Spain refused to sell it. However, Pierce was able to purchase land from Mexico, which gave us our present southwest border, completing our expansion in the West. Pierce was probably grateful when his party neglected to nominate him for another term. At last he could have his privacy.

JAMES BUCHANAN (1791–1868)

Having the distinction of being our only bachelor president, Buchanan did little else to distinguish his administration. Like Fillmore and Pierce he futilely tried to satisfy both North and South in their intensifying conflict. It is one of the ironies of fate—and of politics—that Buchanan, who was a brilliant young lawyer in the 1820s and a promising political figure in the 1830s, should have been passed over when he first sought the presidential nomination in the 1840s, and finally selected to run only when he had become a tired, indecisive old man—until then, the second oldest president ever elected. History has not dealt kindly with "Old Buck," whose record might have looked far better had he never reached the White House. His career as congressman and senator, as minister to Russia and Great Britain, and especially as secretary of state under Polk, earned him a respectable, although far from outstanding, place in history. But he had the misfortune of reaching the nation's highest office well past his prime, at a time of impending crisis. And it was his further misfortune that the remedy of compromise that had in the past at least maintained a surface calm, was no longer sufficient; the problem had outgrown this kind of "solution": the test the nation had been avoiding almost since its beginning was upon it, and the old nostrums simply wouldn't work. Unsure of himself, engrossed in legalistic details, Buchanan pursued a course that history has most dramatically demonstrated to be the wrong one. And it is his unhappy fate to be forever thrust into the shadows by the towering figure of his successor, the man who proved him wrong.

ABRAHAM LINCOLN (1809–65)

A villain to some, a hero to others, Lincoln has undoubtedly attained greatness—but only in retrospect. In all history there is no more dramatic example of the times making a man rather than a man making the times than the legendary rise of Abraham Lincoln from obscurity to the presidency of the shattered Union. Every conceivable obstacle was there before him: humble birth, ignorance, poverty, and life in the wilderness of the frontier; he was completely without advantages or connections; he was too human ever to be a favorite of the professional politicians;

he was too enigmatic, too philosophical, too humorous ever to be a great popular figure. But somehow Lincoln was nominated for the presidency—as the second choice of many; and with less than a majority of the popular vote he managed to be elected in 1860. Out of those early years of poverty and trial emerged a man uniquely prepared to wage a devastating war against many of his former friends and colleagues—a man of haunting transparency, a man with a probing conscience and a penetrating intellect, a man of deep humanity. After the first ineffectual and indecisive eighteen months in office Lincoln became a strong, effective leader—firm, unrelenting, and brutal in the prosecution of both war and politics. But, above all, he proved to be a man of vision. He saw the United States in its largest dimension—as a noble experiment in self-determination that had to be preserved even if that meant violating the principles of self-determination. In the long history of tyranny and oppression, he believed that the American democracy was man's great hope and that it must be saved even if resort had to be made to nondemocratic coercion. To him the great ideal of democracy overshadowed the practical realities of democracy. Lincoln's profound conviction of the enduring value of this experiment in a unified government sustained him throughout the long years of war. On the battlefield at Gettysburg it moved him to give the world a glimpse of his vision of the country's true greatness: "a nation conceived in liberty and dedicated to the proposition that all men are created equal." And it moved him to enunciate his ultimate reason for striving to preserve the Union: that "government of the people, by the people, and for the people shall not perish from the earth." One of the truly great political and human statements of all time, the Gettysburg Address reveals both the ironic complexity and the coarse nobility that mark Lincoln as a legendary figure in American life and culture.

ANDREW JOHNSON (1808–75)

Few men who have reached the presidency have been less prepared for that high office than was Johnson. It is reported that he never spent a single day in a schoolroom. Bound as apprentice to a tailor when only a boy of ten, Johnson spent his youth working long hours in the shop. Only after he had established himself as a tailor in the mountain town of Greenville, Tennessee, and married did he—with the help of his wife—make progress with his education. But, determined as he was, he never achieved the polish of the formally educated. Unfortunately, he also lacked the complex human qualities of his predecessor. But this rough-hewn politician who was plagued with political handicaps of background and personality left his mark on history, for through all his faults and failings shone the kind of integrity and courage that command universal respect. Never in sympathy with the Southern aristocracy, Johnson alone of the twenty-two Southern senators refused to leave his Senate seat in 1861 when his state seceded from the Union. Firm in his resolve, he served the Union as military governor of Tennessee until he was elected vice president in 1864. And after Lincoln's death, the presidency provided him further occasions for courageous action. Fighting the radical Republicans who wanted to grind the war-torn South under the Northern boot, Johnson fearlessly brought the wrath of the Republican Congress on his own head and narrowly missed impeachment—the only president ever to be involved in impeachment proceedings. But he survived that ordeal and, six years after leaving office, he had the pleasure of being elected once again to the Senate, where he had the opportunity to fight against the crushing tyranny of Reconstruction policies put into effect after his tenure in the White House.

ULYSSES S. GRANT (1822–85)

Gen. Ulysses S. Grant was one of the nation's greatest military heroes but one of its most unsuccessful presidents. Decisive and masterful on the battlefield, a dynamic leader and a horseman of great prowess, he proved to be ingenuous in the political arena. Raised on a farm, he early developed a love of horses and seemed always at his best on horseback. As leader of the victorious forces of the North, Grant was considered one of the saviors of the Union. After Johnson's unhappy term, Republicans turned readily to Grant—even though he knew nothing about politics. Innocent and sincere, Grant committed errors of judgment from the beginning: he appointed two unknowns from his home town in Illinois to cabinet positions. Later he allowed himself to be entertained by two stock manipulators—Jay Gould and Jim Fisk—who tried to corner the gold market, a mistake that left him open to charges of incompetence and corruption. As the years passed, the evidences of corruption in his administration were such that Grant lost much of the popularity that first brought him into office. However, he managed to be re-elected to another term, one tarnished by even more corruption, more scandal. In spite of the scandals, Grant scored a few victories. Passage of the Amnesty Bill in 1872 restored civil rights to many Southerners, relieving some of the harsh conditions of Reconstruction. And, against considerable opposition, Grant took courageous steps to fight the growing threat of inflation. But the battle-torn country was still in distress; the general who had brought the great uncivil war to a successful close was not the man to bind up the nation's wounds.

RUTHERFORD B. HAYES (1822–93)

After the scandals of the Grant administration the Republican Party was concerned to choose an especially upright candidate. They found him in Hayes, a devout, conscientious Midwesterner whose Puritan ancestors had come from New England. In his third term as governor of Ohio in 1876, Hayes was known for an honest administration, constructive reforms, and a strong stand on sound money—one of the leading issues of the day. In addition, he had an outstanding

military record—performing gallantly and emerging a major
general. He was apparently above reproach. Yet it is one of
the quirks of history that such a man should reach the
White House through a very questionable settlement of a
disputed election—although most historians believe that
Hayes himself was not personally involved. The settlement
was in the hands of a special electoral commission that happened to have a majority of Republicans. But the Republicans had chosen well—better than some of them knew. For
President Hayes proved to be too honest and forthright for
many of them, who could hardly wait to get him out of
office. Despite political undercurrents, Hayes made good use
of his one term to stabilize the government on several fronts.
He officially ended Reconstruction; he withdrew Federal
troops from the occupied Southern states; he established
reforms in civil service; he took courageous steps to settle the
railroad strike of 1877; and he stood firm in enforcing a
sound money policy—all in the face of vigorous opposition.
The man chosen to remove the taint of scandal from the
government proved to be surprisingly resolute and effective;
his dedication to principle and his courageous and forthright
actions won him the kind of praise earned by very few one-
term presidents.

JAMES A. GARFIELD (1831–81)

He was the last of the presidents to go from a log cabin to
the White House. Left fatherless when only an infant,
Garfield was forced to work from his earliest years on the

family farm in Ohio. Besides helping his widowed
mother, he also succeeded in earning enough—as a canal
boat driver, carpenter, and teacher—to put himself
through college. His love of learning led him into a teaching career—serving as a professor of Latin and Greek and
later a college president. The initiative that catapulted
Garfield into the scholarly ranks ultimately carried him
into public life as well. He became known as a powerful
antislavery speaker and grew active in local politics. A
brilliant career in the Union army—he was a brigadier
general by the time he was thirty—was interrupted when
he resigned after being elected to Congress. There he
served for eighteen years, emerging in 1880 as the leader
of his party. Nevertheless, when the Republicans met in
Chicago in 1880, Garfield was not considered a presidential contender. The struggle was between Grant, who was
willing to try a third term, and Sen. James Blaine from
Maine, but as happened before, the convention was so
divided that neither could win. It was not until the thirty-
sixth ballot that the dark-horse candidate Garfield was
nominated. The surprise gift of the highest office in the
land was not one that Garfield could enjoy for very long.
In the White House he showed signs of being a strong
executive, independent of party as was Hayes. But he was
in office less than four months when he was fatally shot by
an assassin as he was about to catch a train in the
Washington depot on September 19, 1831. Like that earlier log-cabin president, Garfield left the White House a

martyr, having spent less time in office than any president except Harrison.

CHESTER A. ARTHUR (1830–86)

Although the nomination and election of the dark-horse Garfield surprised many Americans, the nomination of Chester Arthur as vice president was even more of a shock. Many a citizen feared the worst when Garfield died with three and a half years of his term remaining. And for good reason. Arthur, who loved fine clothes and elegant living, had been associated with the corrupt New York political machine for almost twenty years. In 1878 he had even been removed from his post as collector of the Port of New York by President Hayes, who had become alarmed at his misuse of patronage. But in spite of his questionable record, Arthur was nominated vice president—largely to appease the powerful party establishment. Thus, when Arthur became president, there was every expectation that the freewheeling spoils system that had reigned in New York would be firmly established in Washington. But Chester Arthur fooled everyone—friends and enemies alike—somehow the responsibilities of that high office seemed to transform this corrupt petty politician into a man sincerely dedicated to the good of the country. Courageously he established his independence by vetoing a graft-laden rivers-and-harbors bill, by breaking with his former machine cronies, and by vigorously prosecuting members of his own party accused of defrauding the government. And, most important, instead of a spoils system, he supported a federal civil service based on competitive examinations and a nonpolitical merit system. By his courageous acts Arthur won over many who had first feared his coming to power, but he lost the support of the political bosses. Although he was not an inspiring leader of men, he earned the nation's gratitude as the champion of the Civil Service system.

GROVER CLEVELAND (1837–1908)

The only man to ever serve two nonconsecutive terms as president, Cleveland performed the greatest comeback in American politics: he succeed his successor. With a limited formal education, Cleveland managed to study law and establish himself as a scrupulously honest office-holder in Buffalo and western New York State. By 1882 his reputation as a dedicated and effective administrator won him the governorship of New York, a post in which he gained further renown by fighting the New York City Democratic machine in cooperation with a young assemblyman, Theodore Roosevelt. "We love him for the enemies he has made," said the delegate nominating Cleveland for the presidency at the 1884 Democratic Convention, for Grover the Crusader had not hesitated to stamp out corruption in his own party. To many of both parties he was the incarnation of clean, honest government. After the corruption, oppression, injustice, and outright tyranny of the Reconstruction era, it was time for a change: "Grover the Good" was elected in 1884, the first Democratic president in twenty-four years. In office Cleveland was a doer—and he continued to make enemies: he made civil service reform a reality by courageously placing a number of political jobs under the protection of civil service, and he stood firmly against a high protective tariff, moves that contributed to his defeat in 1888. While out of office Cleveland assumed the role of party spokesman and became an active critic of the Harrison administration. In 1892 he soundly defeated the man who had replaced him in the White House. But he returned to power in grim times with a depression cutting deep into the nation's economy; strong measures were called for, and in forcing repeal of silver legislation and halting the Pullman labor strike, Cleveland demonstrated a firm hand. Throughout a difficult term he remained an honest, independent leader, a man who left office with the hard-won respect of members of both parties.

BENJAMIN HARRISON (1833–1901)

Grandson of a president and great-grandson of a signer of the Declaration of Independence, Benjamin Harrison carried a distinguished American name into the White House, but most historians generally agree that he added very little distinction to it during his stay there. Harrison's early years were filled with promise and success—admitted to the Indiana bar at the age of twenty, he became one of the state's ablest lawyers, and he interrupted his law career only to become a brigadier general for the Union army in the War Between the States at the age of thirty-two. But the success that marked his early years was rather spotty when he entered politics after the war. Shortly after returning to Indiana he was defeated running for governor. After one term in the U.S. Senate he failed to be re-elected in 1887. And his victory over Cleveland in the presidential election of 1888 was matched by a defeat at his hands when the two ran against each other in 1892. Although he performed bravely on the battlefield, Harrison was not a bold president. Strongly supported and influenced by the mammoth trusts and other business interests, he signed into law one of the highest protective tariffs the country has ever known; and even when a bill to curb the trusts—the Sherman Anti-Trust Act—managed to be passed, his administration did virtually nothing to enforce it. In spite of such concessions to big business, the economy grew worse. Harrison permitted the country's gold reserves to be severely depleted by a questionable pension plan for war veterans. By the close of his administration the signs of depression had multiplied. As is almost always the case, what was good for the huge corporate trusts had not proved to be good for the nation. The cautious man who was afraid of the new electric lights in the White House had failed to convince the country that he could lead on to better times: once again the country turned to Cleveland.

WILLIAM MCKINLEY (1843–1901)

Although a kind, gentle man beloved by the American people, McKinley did not earn a place in history as a champion of the people. Instead, his administration was closely identified with monopolies, trusts, corporations, and special interests. At a time when the expanding West and the agrarian South were developing populist movements of growing political significance, the dignified Midwestern lawyer represented the bankers, mercantilists, and industrialists who formed the most powerful bloc in the Republican Party establishment. Both economically and politically, McKinley was a conservative; on the three burning issues of the day—the tariff, currency, and Cuba—he took a conservative position. The McKinley Tariff Bill, passed in 1890, was one of the highest protective tariffs in U.S. history. As president, McKinley supported the gold standard and for a time resisted those who wanted to stampede the United States into war with Spain to rescue an oppressed Cuba. McKinley had been elected on a platform supporting Cuban independence. American investments in sugar plantations and trade with Cuba were at stake, and the newspapers kept stories of Spanish atrocities in Cuba before the eyes of the public. The pressure for American intervention—after the sinking of the battle cruiser *Maine* in Havana Harbor—finally moved McKinley to go to war. The remarkable victories of servicemen like Teddy Roosevelt on the field and Dewey on the seas brought Puerto Rico, Guam, and the Philippines into American hands. Ironically, the conservative McKinley launched the nation as a global power. With McKinley's reelection in 1900 big business seemed secure for four more years. But a series of accidents dramatically altered this serene picture. In the 1900 campaign the progressive governor of New York, Theodore Roosevelt, was put on the ticket as vice president by rival New York Republican leaders who hoped that post would be his political graveyard. But only six months after the inauguration McKinley was fatally shot by an anarchist at the Pan-American Exposition in Buffalo on September 14, 1901. And the era of freewheeling big business died with McKinley, the third martyred president.

THEODORE ROOSEVELT (1858–1919)

Before his fiftieth birthday he had served as a New York state legislator, the undersecretary of the navy, police commissioner for the city of New York, U.S. Civil Service commissioner, the governor of New York, the vice president under William McKinley, a colonel in the U.S. Army, and two terms as the president of the United States. In addition, he had run a cattle ranch in the Dakota Territories, served as a reporter and editor for several journals, newspapers, and magazines, and conducted scientific expeditions on four continents. He read at least five books every week of his life and wrote nearly fifty on an astonishing array of subjects—from history and biography to natural science and social criticism. He enjoyed hunting, boxing, and wrestling. He was an amateur taxidermist, botanist, ornithologist, and astronomer. He was a devoted family man who lovingly raised six children. And he enjoyed a lifelong romance with his wife. During his long and varied career he was hailed by supporters and rivals alike as the greatest man of the age—perhaps one of the greatest of all ages. A reformer and fighter, he was the most colorful and the most controversial president since Lincoln, the most versatile since Jefferson. Born to wealth, Roosevelt was imbued with a strong sense of public service; in every position he held, he fought for improvement and reform. His was largely a moral crusade: he saw his chief enemy as non-Christian corruption and weakness, and he vigorously fought it wherever he found it—in business or in government. In the White House the many-sided personality of Roosevelt captured the American imagination. The youngest man to become president, this dynamic reformer who combined a Harvard accent with the toughness of a Dakota cowboy was a totally new kind of president. Fighting the "malefactors of great wealth," Roosevelt struck out against the mammoth trusts that appeared to be outside government regulation. The railroads, the food and drug industries, and enterprises using the natural wealth of the public lands all were subjected to some form of regulation, for the protection of the public interest. Many conservation practices began with Roosevelt. A reformer at home, he was an avowed expansionist abroad. He supported the Spanish War and led his "Rough Riders" to fame; when president, he acquired the Canal Zone from Panama and sent U.S. battleships on a world cruise—to show off America's growing strength. Perhaps most notable were Roosevelt's efforts to end the Russo-Japanese War, an achievement that won him the Nobel Peace Prize. But this peacemaker, soldier, explorer, hunter, scientist, writer and progressive statesman left many a mark upon history: to government he brought the fresh winds of reform, and the courage, vigor, and tenacity to make his reforms an enduring part of the American scene.

WILLIAM H. TAFT (1857–1930)

Most Americans were saddened—although the Republican establishment was relieved—when Roosevelt announced he would not seek a third term. His successor was the country's largest president, a jovial, warm-hearted mountain of a man with a brilliant legal mind—an excellent administrator but a poor politician. He served with distinction as the first governor of the Philippines and as Roosevelt's secretary of war, positions in which his amiable nature served to advantage. But it was Taft's great misfortune to succeed such a dazzling political figure as Roosevelt in the presidency and attempt to carry out his many new policies. Probably no successor could have pleased Roosevelt, but the fall from grace of the devoted friend Roosevelt had practically placed in the White House is one of the most tragic affairs in the history of the presidency. Near the end of Taft's administration, when it was clear that he had not completely supported Roosevelt's Square Deal and had made concessions to the conservatives, Roosevelt fiercely attacked him in speeches and articles. In the 1912 election Roosevelt won every primary and was poised to sweep back into office when the Republican establishment stripped the credentials of hundreds of delegates and denied the great man the opportunity. They renominated the compliant Taft instead.

Roosevelt helped to organize the Progressive Party and nearly won the day anyway. With less than a month to go in the campaign, however, a nearly successful assassination took Roosevelt out of the race and the Democratic opponent, Woodrow Wilson, was able to barely eke out a win. Taft and the bosses of the Republican Party establishment were humiliated. In spite of that, Taft continued to serve his country. After teaching law at Yale he was appointed by President Harding to the post that he had long sought, one that probably meant more to him than the presidency: in 1921 he became chief justice of the Supreme Court, the only man ever to hold both offices.

WOODROW WILSON (1856–1924)

Although Wilson held only one political office before he became president, his years as a professor of history provided him with a detailed knowledge of political processes; as president of Princeton University and governor of New Jersey he proved himself an able, dedicated administrator, unafraid to institute reforms. Thus Wilson's philosophy, knowledge, and ability uniquely equipped him for the nation's highest office. It was ironic then that his policies were, for the most part, dictated by a secretive band of political cronies led by a man named Colonel House.

The administration's misguided conspiratorial energies were first directed toward domestic issues: a lower tariff, stronger antitrust measures, a child-labor law, the first income-tax law, and the Federal Reserve Act—the last greatly centralizing the economy and the control of money through the establishment of a semiprivate national bank. But the country that had emerged as a world power under McKinley and Roosevelt could not long ignore the conflict in Europe. Wilson kept the country out of war during his first term, but America's sympathy with the Allies made his ostensible neutrality difficult to maintain. "To make the world safe for democracy," Wilson finally led the nation into war in 1917. In directing the war effort Wilson cooperated with a Congress that gave him vast emergency powers. While mobilizing the industrial as well as the military forces of the nation, he labored over plans for peace—his great hope was for a kind of multinational government called the League of Nations. But his dedication to the noble ideal of the League's Covenant led to a bitter conflict with Congress when the Covenant, already signed by the European powers, was before them for approval. When Congress rejected it, he suffered his greatest defeat. During the last several months of his administration, he was deathly ill and his cronies practically ran what they could of the government as their personal fiefdom.

WARREN G. HARDING (1865–1923)

Promising a nation weary of war and of big-government social experiments "a return to normalcy," the good-natured, undistinguished senator from Ohio was swept into office in 1920. Harding, the dark-horse Republican candidate, received over seven million votes more than the Democrat

James Cox, who ran on Wilson's dismal record. The genial Harding had run on Theodore Roosevelt's platform pledging "not heroics, but healing; not nostrums, but normalcy." The editor of a small-town newspaper, Harding was an easygoing politician who seemed to be everybody's friend. In the eyes of his clever manager, Harry Daugherty, Harding had one great asset: he looked like a president. Handsome, with dignified bearing and easy charm, Harding was an impressive figure, and it was as a figurehead, as ceremonial chief of state, that he best filled the office of president. He was the first "packaged" president—although certainly not the last. Neither a leader nor a man of ideas, he seemed to represent the mood and temper of the McKinley administration rather than the two decades of progressive government that had followed; high protective tariffs were established, and both the regulation and taxation of business were reduced. Once again the government seemed to be at the service of the privileged few. Ironically, with the return to "normalcy" came rumors of corruption in high places—at the cabinet level. Daugherty, who had become attorney general, was later discovered to have freely sold his influence, and Secretary of the Interior Albert Fall was eventually convicted for accepting $100,000 from private oil interests. But the public—as well as the president himself—knew nothing of these scandals in the summer of 1923 when Harding took a trip to Alaska. Harding learned the details on his return trip. And then he died under very suspicious conditions in San Francisco only a few days later. The country mourned the passing of the warm-hearted man who had symbolized the tranquil, prewar America, perhaps sensing that such "normalcy" was as irrevocably lost as was their president.

CALVIN COOLIDGE (1872–1933)

The sixth vice president to reach the White House through the death of a president, Coolidge differed markedly from the man he succeeded. Harding was easygoing and chatty, Coolidge shy and reserved. Harding an inexperienced executive, Coolidge a proven administrator. Harding was a man ruled by few defined principles; Coolidge was a taciturn Yankee with a passion for economy and efficiency. But both believed in less rather than more government; both favored business. "The business of America is business," said Coolidge, in a statement as long as almost any he made. Somehow the pious, businesslike Coolidge was never associated with the scandals of Harding's administration, and he managed to establish his own tenure as thoroughly honest and efficient. In every position he held—from mayor of Northampton, Massachusetts, to vice president—he demonstrated what he meant by efficient government by working long hours himself. "We need more of the office desk and less of the show window in politics." The times were good, business prospered, the size and cost of government were cut drastically, and the industrious New Englander in the White House gained public favor. In 1924 the country showed its approval by electing him for another term. In the years that followed he continued to effect economies in government. In August 1927, with character-istic brevity, he announced, "I do not choose to run for President in 1928." Although by now enormously popular, no one could change his mind. The man who had worked to maintain stability was determined to leave the White House while the country was enjoying stable and prosperous times.

HERBERT HOOVER (1874–1964)

He was one of those men—like both of the Adamses, Jefferson, and Madison—whose greatest contribution to the nation was not made in the White House. For Hoover, an extraordinarily successful mining engineer and administrator, the presidency was a time of trial—he was elected on a prosperity platform during the 1928 boom, but the stock market crash and the grinding depression that followed proved to be harsh contradictions to his innate optimism. Orphaned at nine, Hoover learned the Quaker virtues and rewards of hard work at an early age. He put himself through the first class at Stanford and became a phenomenal success as a mining engineer before he was thirty. Known and respected in international mining circles, he gained worldwide fame when he directed emergency relief activities in Europe during the First World War. By the end of that terrible conflict he held a unique place in the eyes of the world as a dedicated administrator in the service of the cause of humanity. Success continued to be Hoover's lot when he served as secretary of commerce in the Harding and Coolidge cabinets, where he re-organized and expanded the Commerce Department. Running against the popular governor of New York, Alfred E. Smith, in 1928, Hoover was again successful, gaining more popular votes than any previous candidate. But when Hoover took office, vast forces were at work: the stock market collapsed, the booming industrial complex of the United States broke down, and no individual—not even Hoover with all the powers of the presidency—could cope with the disaster. He instituted measures to stimulate business with government aid, but the depression continued throughout his years in office. He was overwhelmingly defeated running for reelection in 1932.

FRANKLIN D. ROOSEVELT (1882–1945)

There are two figures that dominated the American political scene in the twentieth century. The first was Theodore Roosevelt. The second, remarkably, was his young cousin, Franklin. Both men possessed great personal charisma, keen political instincts, penetrating social consciences, seemingly boundless energy, and brilliantly diverse intellects. Both of them left a lasting impression upon the world in which we live. But that is where the similarity between the two ends. In every other way, they could not have been more different. Franklin was the patriarch of the Hyde Park side of the family. A Harvard-educated lawyer, he began his political career as a Democratic Party reformer in the New York state senate. His vigorous campaign on behalf of Wilson—against his famous cousin—during the 1912 presidential election earned him an appointment as assistant secretary of the navy. In 1920 he was the vice presidential running mate on the losing Democratic ticket. Eight years later, after a crippling bout with polio, he was elected to the first of two terms as New York's governor. Finally, in 1932 he ran for the presidency against the Great Depression–plagued Herbert Hoover and won overwhelmingly. During his record four terms he directed the ambitious transformation of American government, created the modern system of social welfare, guided the nation through World War II, and laid the foundations for the United Nations. Theodore Roosevelt was a conservative social reformer who wanted to firmly and faithfully reestablish the "Old World Order." Franklin on the other hand, was a liberal social revolutionary who wanted to boldly and unashamedly usher in the "New World Order." Theodore's motto was "Speak softly and carry a big stick." Franklin's motto was "Good neighbors live in solidarity." Both men understood the very critical notion that ideas have consequences. As a result, the twentieth century in America has largely been the tale of two households—of the Roosevelts of Sagamore Hill and the Roosevelts of Hyde Park. In his tenure in office, Franklin introduced far-reaching social and economic changes in the form and function of government to stimulate the economy and relieve the distress of millions of unemployed. In thus extending the influence of the federal government farther than ever before into the social and economic lives of the country, he transformed the republic from limited representationalism to bureaucratic interventionism. The only president to serve more than two terms, Roosevelt was reelected in 1936, 1940, and 1944. Domestic problems dominated his first term, but by the middle of the second, he began to recognize the aggressiveness of the Axis powers as a serious threat to world peace. Roosevelt offered American aid to the Allied powers and, after the attack on Pearl Harbor, he directed the greatest total war effort—military and civilian—in all history. Supposedly to make America "the arsenal of democracy," the government took on war powers to regulate every aspect of industrial production and civilian consumption—thus, America was ruled with much of the same centralized control as the rest of the nations of the earth during the difficult days of the Second World War. Although already ailing, Roosevelt met with Churchill and Stalin at Teheran in 1943 to plan strategy, and in 1945 at Yalta to plan for peace. Roosevelt was in Warm Springs, Georgia, preparing a speech for the San Francisco United Nations Conference when he died suddenly.

HARRY S. TRUMAN (1884–1972)

In succeeding to the office that Roosevelt held through twelve years of depression, world tension, and war, Truman faced the greatest challenge ever to confront an American vice president. Thrust without warning into the role of world leader, he was immediately burdened with two almost overwhelming tasks—leading the nation to final victory in the war and planning a sound world peace. Truman emerged from the shadow of his predecessor, dealt courageously with these problems, and in 1948 established himself as president in his own right when he upset all predictions by defeating Gov. Thomas E. Dewey of New York. As a young man Truman had done farming, served in the First World War as an artillery captain, and been partner in a haberdashery; in 1929 he entered politics. After studying law and serving as county judge, he was elected to the Senate in 1934. During the Second World War the Truman Committee became known for its careful investigation of defense spending; Harry Truman won national prominence and, in 1944, the vice presidential nomination. Truman's administration was filled with momentous events: in the first year he met with Churchill and Stalin at Potsdam; he made the historic decision to use the atomic bomb; Germany and Japan surrendered; and America accepted the United Nations' Charter. In the following years came the Marshall Plan—with aid for Europe; aid and technical assistance for underdeveloped countries; the establishment of NATO; and in 1950 the Korean War—the most dramatic step the nation had taken to try to contain Communism. Sending troops to Korea to fight a "limited" war and deciding to use the atomic bomb represented totally new kinds of decisions for a president; in making them, the man who said "The buck stops here" forced the country face to face with the two greatest problems of the day—nuclear power and the threat of Communism.

DWIGHT D. EISENHOWER (1890–1969)

He was the popular hero of the Second World War and thus was drafted by the Republican Party to run for president in 1952. In that year the genial "Ike," whose apparent sincerity and goodwill captured the country, took his place with other American military heroes who have been elevated to the presidency. Like Zachary Taylor and Ulysses Grant, Eisenhower was a professional soldier who had never held a political office. In the army Eisenhower distinguished himself in planning and staff work; during the 1930s he served as special assistant to Gen. Douglas MacArthur and aided him when he became military adviser to the Philippines. During the Second World War, Eisenhower commanded the North African invasion and later became famous as the man who devised the D-Day invasion and then welded the armies of the Allied nations into a mighty force that eventually won the war against the Nazis. Elected on a platform of peace, Eisenhower used the powers of the presidency to reduce world tension: his first year in office he brought the Korean War to an end, and after both American and Russian scientists developed hydrogen bombs, he proposed an "open-skies" plan for disarmament, as well as plans for an international atom pool for peaceful use. Despite such efforts, the problem of containing Communism continued to be a major concern throughout his administration: the Communists took North Vietnam in 1954, and in 1956 Russian troops reconquered a fighting Hungary that had struggled heroically to win its brief moment of freedom. The enormous popularity that carried Eisenhower into the White House remained undiminished in 1956, when he again defeated Adlai Stevenson of Illinois. During his second term, racial segregation became a consuming domestic issue, one that reached a climax in September 1957, when he sent troops to Little Rock, Arkansas, to ensure safety to black schoolchildren. With the Communist threat continuing to dominate the world scene, Eisenhower made a dramatic world tour for peace. In 1961, when he retired to his Gettysburg farm, the nation had reached a state of unparalleled prosperity.

JOHN F. KENNEDY (1917–1963)

The youngest man ever elected president—and the youngest to die in office—Kennedy defeated Vice President Richard Nixon in the first presidential election that featured candidates in formal television debates before millions of voters across the nation. A naval hero during the Second World War, he was the first Catholic to be elected president. Kennedy was born into a family with a political history—both his grandfathers were active in politics, and his father served as the nation's ambassador to Great Britain. But Kennedy first won acclaim as an author when his Harvard honors thesis, published as *Why*

England Slept, became a best seller. In the war he was decorated for saving his PT-boat crew when a Japanese destroyer cut his boat in two. In 1946 he entered politics and was elected to Congress from Massachusetts. Six years later he became a senator. Publication of Kennedy's book *Profiles in Courage*—which won the Pulitzer prize despite the fact that it was ghostwritten—coincided with his emergence on the national political scene. In 1956 he narrowly missed the Democratic nomination for vice president; by 1960 he was a leading contender for the presidency. He defeated Nixon in one of the closest elections in the nation's history—less than one vote per precinct separated them. On taking office, Kennedy delivered a stirring Inaugural Address—written by the same ghosts who had garnered his literary fame—he appealed to all peoples for restraint and cooperation in building a safe and free world in the age of nuclear weapons. In his first year he introduced a number of new social welfare programs, weathered the Bay of Pigs disaster, and met Communist challenges throughout the world. His space program bore fruit in 1962 when Astronaut John Glenn orbited the earth. By challenging the Communist buildup in Cuba, Kennedy effected the first significant Russian retreat of the Cold War. In 1963 he reached an agreement with Russia to limit nuclear tests and offered controversial civil rights and tax bills to Congress. Before Congress acted, on November 22, while President Kennedy was in Dallas, Texas, on a speaking tour with his wife, he was assassinated by a sniper—a tragedy that shocked the world.

LYNDON B. JOHNSON (1908–1973)

He was the eighth vice president to take the place of a president who died in office, and the fourth to be elected to a new term. One of the most experienced national political figures ever elected vice president, he was sworn into office in Dallas, shortly after President Kennedy was assassinated. Like his predecessor, Johnson was born into a family with a political heritage—his father and grandfather were both in politics. Indeed, when he was born, his grandfather predicted he would be a U.S. senator. By the time he was forty, Johnson had achieved what his grandfather had predicted—although the manipulative means by which he did remained a scandal throughout his career. In the Senate his abilities to lead and persuade made themselves felt; as Senate Majority Leader during President Eisenhower's administrations, Johnson established himself as a skillful and commanding political leader. He provided the Republican president bipartisan support for such critical legislation as the civil rights bill that was passed in 1957, the first civil rights legislation in more than eighty years. In 1960 Johnson surprised many political friends when he ran as vice president on the Kennedy ticket. After becoming president, he moved firmly to stabilize the government and to support Kennedy programs at home and abroad. In November 1964, Johnson won a landslide election that pitted his own New Deal liberalism against Sen. Barry Goldwater's conservatism. In 1965 he sent Congress his programs to build "The Great Society." One of the most productive in congressional history, that session turned into law bills on Medicare, school and college aid, voting rights, and anti-poverty measures. During 1965 Johnson also increased the nation's commitment in Vietnam and, in December, directed the first air raid against North Vietnam. The bombing and the continued increases of troops in Vietnam led to large, occasionally violent demonstrations. The country was also torn by riots in predominantly Negro sections of major cities. On March 31, 1968, President Johnson stunned the nation by announcing he would not run for re-election. In October he announced a bombing halt that led to more serious peace talks in Paris. The closing days of his administration saw a flawless Apollo flight to the moon and indications from the Paris talks of improved prospects for peace in Vietnam.

RICHARD M. NIXON (1918–1995)

The first president to resign from office, Nixon removed himself from the presidency August 9, 1974, after it became clear that he could not survive the impeachment proceedings then in progress. One month later he was granted an unqualified pardon by his successor. It was an ignominious end to a rather spectacular political career. He first won national attention in 1948 when, as a member of the House Un-American Activities Committee, he forced the confrontation that led to the perjury conviction of Alger Hiss. As vice president in 1959, he conducted the famous "kitchen debate" with the Russian dictator Nikita Khrushchev in Moscow. He was defeated for the presidency by Kennedy in 1960 but after a seven-year absence, he returned to national office in 1968 when he defeated Vice President Hubert Humphrey to finally attain that office. During his first term, an American became the first man to walk on the moon, opposition to U.S. participation in Vietnam took the form of mass demonstrations all across the nation, and the Soviet Union entered into strategic arms limitations talks. Most significant were Nixon's efforts to resolve international problems and promote world peace—he was a brilliant foreign policy expert. In February 1972 he became the first president ever to visit Communist China. His talks with Premier Chou En-lai and Chairman Mao Tse-tung led to a historic agreement pledging peaceful coexistence. In May 1972 Nixon and Chairman Brezhnev of the Soviet Union signed a treaty that reduced antiballistic missile deployment and limited the number of offensive strategic weapons—the first significant action to limit the nuclear arms race. But, on June 17, 1972, four men were arrested for breaking into the Democratic National Headquarters in the Watergate office building complex. Nixon and his aides denied involvement, and they succeeded in convincing the nation, so that the incident was not a significant issue in the 1972 election, which Nixon easily won. In 1973 he began withdrawing all troops from Vietnam. During the next eighteen months, the Senate Watergate hearings, the revelation of the White House tapes, the trials of more than twenty Nixon aides, and, finally, the Supreme Court's 8–0 decision forcing Nixon to surrender crucial tapes to the special prosecutor, convinced him that he faced impeachment if he did not resign.

GERALD R. FORD (1913–)

America's first unelected president, Ford assumed the office of president August 9, 1974, when President Nixon resigned. Eight months before, Ford had become the first appointed vice president. He was the first to assume both positions under the provisions of the Constitution's Amendment 25. An exceptional football player at the University of Michigan, Ford coached football at Yale while studying law there. In the Second World War he served as a naval officer in the Pacific. In 1948 he won a seat in Congress and soon gained a reputation for his ability to deal with the complexities of defense budgets. Over the next two decades he built a record that was moderate to conservative. During those years he declined to run for both the governorship and the Senate—preferring to remain in the House. In 1960 he won the position of GOP conference chairman. Two years later he was elected minority leader. Ford began his presidency with immense popular support. His sudden pardon of Nixon, though, brought sharp criticism. On taking office, he stated he would not be a candidate in 1976, but in July 1975 he reversed himself and announced he would run. That year he signed the Helsinki accords with the Soviets and thirty other nations, and met with Chinese leaders in Peking, seeking to maintain stable, if limited, relations. By early 1976 it was clear that Ford had succeeded in bringing the country out of the recession, and his "peace and prosperity" campaign brought him early primary victories. But, although he presided over a glorious Bicentennial Fourth of July and the economic recovery continued, he narrowly defeated Reagan for the party's nomination. Although the nation's economic recovery slowed during the campaign and Democratic candidate Carter dominated the first presidential television debates since 1960, Ford came from behind to make a very close race of the election. Ford was the first incumbent since Herbert Hoover to lose a presidential election.

JAMES E. CARTER (1924–)

In only the second presidential election involving nationally televised debates, Carter came from comparative obscurity to capture the Democratic nomination and the presidency, the first man from the Deep South elected president since before the War Between the States. As a young naval officer, he served in the nuclear submarine program under Adm. Hyman Rickover. After his father died, Carter resigned from the navy and returned to Georgia to operate the family farm. His father had served in the Georgia senate, and Carter's first public service was on the local school board. In 1967, as a little-known candidate, he defeated an experienced state senator, winning a disputed election in which his opponent used illegal tactics. In 1966 Carter ran for the Democratic nomination for governor, but lost to Lester Maddox; in 1970 he was elected. Carter's presidency was marked by a continuing commitment to human rights, a quest for Arab-Israeli peace, and, at the end, an interminable hostage crisis. In 1977 Carter proposed a comprehensive Energy Program—calling the problem "the moral equivalent of war," created a new Energy Department, and signed the controversial treaties that relinquished control of the Panama Canal. In 1978 Carter helped bring Egypt's Anwar Sadat and Israel's Menachem Begin to agree on the historic Camp David Accords, establishing a "framework for peace" in the Middle East. In 1979 he established diplomatic relations with Communist China and ended relations with Taiwan. That year world oil prices more than doubled and inflation soared to double digits. The Iranian seizure of Americans at the embassy in Tehran in November 1979 created a crisis that dominated the nation's concerns until they were released almost a year and a half later. To protest the Soviet invasion of Afghanistan, Carter instituted a grain and trade embargo and enforced a boycott of the 1980 Olympics in Moscow. Although he proclaimed himself a "born again" Christian, he was a committed supporter of abortion on demand, radical feminism, and homosexual advocacy. Carter barely survived the challenge of Sen. Edward Kennedy for his party's nomination, but in the election he was roundly defeated by Republican Ronald Reagan.

RONALD W. REAGAN (1911–)

Twice winning landslide elections—by the greatest electoral margin since Franklin Roosevelt defeated Alfred Landon in 1936—Reagan ushered in a new era of conservatism and traditionalism after the long tenure of liberals in the highest office in the land. A comparative latecomer to politics, Reagan achieved national recognition as a leading man in more than four dozen Hollywood movies and as a network television host. He served six terms as president of the Screen Actors Guild and two terms as president of the Motion Picture Industry Council. He emerged suddenly on the national political scene in 1964 when he delivered a rousing speech on television supporting presidential candidate Barry Goldwater. Two years later he was elected governor of California. Reagan's victory over incumbent Jimmy Carter in 1980 represented a profound political shift toward conservatism across the country. In Washington, on March 30, 1981, President Reagan was wounded in an assassination attempt. After successful surgery he was able to continue to function as president. That year he won Congressional approval of a tax cut and appointed the first woman—Sandra O'Connor—to the Supreme Court. After a recession in 1982, the U.S. economy began a remarkably strong recovery that endured to the end of his second term.

After his landslide victory in 1984—won in large part because he had mobilized the emerging Religious Right—he continued to set a conservative pace, including a tax-reform bill and a strong defense system. His strong opposition to terrorism and Communism—including the bombing of Libya, the liberation of Grenada, and tough economic pressures on the Soviet bloc—won general approval at home, criticism abroad. His meetings with the new leader of the Soviet Union, Mikhail Gorbachev, in 1985 and 1988, led to historic agreements on the banning of intermediate-range nuclear missiles. The American economy continued to expand—but the federal government's budget deficit soared to unprecedented heights. Reagan left office the most popular president since Theodore Roosevelt.

GEORGE BUSH (1924–)

The first incumbent vice president since Martin Van Buren to be elected president, Bush defeated Democratic candidate Michael Dukakis, governor of Massachusetts, by a landslide—by essentially riding on President Reagan's coat tails and by reinforcing his party's ties to the Religious Right. Although his election provided continuity to the conservative "Reagan Revolution," the Democratic Party remained securely in control of Congress. Bush came to the presidency with extensive experience in government and politics, having served in Congress, and in the military, diplomatic, and intelligence arms of the executive branch, and as chairman of the Republican National Committee, before becoming vice president. His father, Prescott Bush, was U.S. senator from Connecticut from 1952 to 1962. In 1942, at age eighteen, Bush volunteered for service as a naval pilot, becoming the youngest in the navy. He flew fifty-eight combat missions in the Pacific during the Second World War. He was shot down—but was later rescued by an American submarine. After the war he took his degree at Yale in three years—and captained the baseball team. He first entered politics in 1962. Working in Houston in the oil business, he was elected chairman of the Harris County Republican Party. Two years later he ran an unsuccessful campaign for the Senate. In 1968, while serving his first term in Congress, he faced a crisis when he voted for an open-housing bill that many of his white constituents opposed. His speech in Houston defending his vote won him support, and he was reelected. However, in running for the Senate in 1970, he lost to Democrat Lloyd Bentsen. Over the next decade Bush represented the United States at the United Nations and in China, and served as director of the Central Intelligence Agency. He campaigned for the presidency in 1980 but settled for vice president under Ronald Reagan. Although he had won office as the heir to the Reagan Revolution, he quietly betrayed the basic principles of that grassroots conservative groundswell—he reluctantly supported major tax increases, did little to effectively deal with core moral issues, and allowed the budget deficit to continue to soar. He gained immense popularity between 1989 and 1991 when the old Soviet bloc began to fall apart and Communism lost power. That popularity was enhanced even more when the Gulf War against Iraq's incursions into Kuwait proved overwhelmingly successful. But his weak domestic policy and his unwillingness to maintain the core support of conservatives and the Religious Right cost him the 1992 election.

WILLIAM JEFFERSON CLINTON (1946–)

Attaining the highest office in the land despite losing more than 57 percent of the electoral vote, Clinton's tenure in the White House got off to a controversial start when on his first day in office he institutionalized aggressive abortion and homosexual rights policies. Thus he quickly plunged into the heated "culture war" debates that were already raging throughout the nation. Nevertheless, his remarkable political skills enabled him to maintain extraordinary approval ratings, overcome a series of scandals, and eventually gain reelection—a first for any Democrat since Franklin Roosevelt. Rising from poverty and a broken home, he made his mark in academia and ultimately became a Rhodes scholar. In 1977, just five years out of school, he was elected attorney general of Arkansas. Two years later he was elected governor of the state. His progressive idealism proved to be a bit much for the conservative state, and he was defeated in 1981 during his reelection bid. During the next two years he reinvented himself and with his new image was able to convince the electorate that he had changed. He won back the governorship—and held it for four more terms. Then, overcoming a spate of lurid rumors and minor scandals, he won the Democratic nomination for president in 1992. The general election later that year was marked by a good deal of apathy, malaise, and a massive defection from the two major parties—more than twenty-one million votes went to third-party candidates. Clinton's lack of an electoral mandate was highlighted by the defeat of his health care reform plan—designed by his powerful first lady, Hillary Rodham Clinton. His setback in the 1994 elections when his party lost its majority tenure in both the House and the Senate for the first time in a half century seemed to bode ill for his reelection chances. Nevertheless, exploiting the Republicans' lack of decisive leadership, his extraordinary political instincts enabled him not only to win election to a second term but to overcome impeachment for perjury following a spate of lurid scandals and to survive a series of foreign policy debacles. Thus, despite ending his term of office in disgrace, he proved himself to be a consummate politician.